SPECIAL

THE OPEN MEDIA PAMPHLET SERIES

EDITION

OTHER OPEN MEDIA PAMPHLET SERIES TITLES

10 Reasons to Abolish the IMF & World Bank

KEVIN DANAHER

Foreword by Anuradha Mittal

Series editor Greg Ruggiero

SEVEN STORIES PRESS / NEW YORK

CONTENTS

ACKNOWLEDGMENTS

This book evolved out of a public lecture I have delivered to many different audiences over the past few years. I would like to thank all the participants who raised questions, objections, and clarifications that added to the arguments contained herein.

My deepest thanks to my many comrades at Global Exchange who make it fun to come to work every day. Special thanks to Greg Ruggiero at Seven Stories Press for a frictionless relationship working on this project.

This book is dedicated to sweet, tough, smart Maya. The best daughter any dad could have.

The tragic events of September 11, 2001, changed the world forever. The violence in Washington and New York could have disastrous ramifications for the United States and the entire world. If the Bush administration unleashes destruction on innocent people it will breed more terrorism and the descending spiral of violence could devour what is best in American society.

Americans have been noted for ignoring the impact of U.S. foreign policy. That ignorance has often been expensive for foreigners, especially the poor, who get hurt by U.S. economic and military policies. But it is now obvious that Americans can also suffer from their ignorance of U.S. foreign policy.

This book was conceived as an effort to educate the general public about the secret global government being constructed behind the backs of the citizens of the planet. The World Bank and the International Monetary Fund, along with the World Trade Organization, are making policy for the entire bouquet of humanity but with only a monocrop (the wealthy) sitting at the rule-making table. We argue for a democratization of the process by which economic policy making takes places.

Now it is obvious that we need to democratize the process of enforcing international law as well. The huge decision confronting Americans is this: do we define the violence of September 11 as an act of war or as a crime against humanity. If we define it as war, it couches the issues in nationalist rhetoric and emphasizes our differences with the people of other nations. If we define it as a crime against humanity it holds the potential for uniting humankind against the scourge of terrorism.

Whatever course events may take, global governance (in the economic realm, the justice realm, and the military realm) is still the central topic before us. The same points we have been making in favor of democratizing economic policy on the planet apply just as strongly to the justice/police/military realm.

The Growing Movement Against Economic Warfare

by Anuradha Mittal

Signboards at the Singapore airport greet visitors with the message, "Capitalists of the World Unite." The collapse of the Socialist bloc and the end of the Cold War have been interpreted as the victory of global capitalism. We have been told that economic globalization, brought about by the free reign of the market, is benign, and that it brings the greatest good for the greatest number. Nation states are being increasingly directed to get out of the way of market forces and let the synergy between the technological revolution and big business reshape the world. And this will take care of those in need of food, medicine, and work in the Third World.

Global corporatization, promoted through trade agreements, has thrived on these arguments and has ushered in an era of promise and uncertainty. While it has accelerated the accumulation of wealth for some, most working poor have been left behind and inequalities within and among nations have grown.

In Southern countries demands for jobs, decent livelihoods, land, water, and food security have reached a new crescendo. For millions of small farmers, fisherfolk, and indigenous peoples, trade liberalization has deprived them of access to and control over natural resources and denied their basic human right to an adequate standard of living.

Yet the nations of the South are not the only victims of this process. There is also a "South in the North" in "developed countries" like the United States where the working class has been harmed by the trade agreements. Since NAFTA was signed on January 1, 1994, the United States has suffered a net loss attributable to trade of about 400,000 industrial jobs and hundreds of thousands of jobs in the manufacturing sector. These were largely union jobs with decent pay and benefits. Typically those displaced, who found new jobs, get paid only 70 percent of their former salaries. A study by Cornell professor Kate Bronfenbrenner found that since the passage of NAFTA, 71 percent of U.S. industrial employers threatened to close the factory if workers formed a union. Bronfenbrenner found evidence that these threats had their desired effect, reducing the rate of success in union organizing drives.

This belief in the "market" threatens to set narrow limits to human aspirations in coming decades. Far reaching economic decisions are made during meetings of the World Economic Forum, G-8, World Bank, and the IMF. These meetings are shrouded in secrecy, carried out in a distinctly non-transparent and cavalier way in which crucial decisions are made with little or no participation from those likely to be negatively affected by their outcome.

So who is running this show?

ENGINES OF ECONOMIC GLOBALIZATION

The key international financial institutions called by many the "Unholy Trinity," are the WTO, the International Monetary Fund (IMF), and the World Bank. Founded in 1944, the IMF has promoted ever freer global capital flows while the World Bank has supervised the transformation of developing countries along free market lines and managed their integration into the world economy. These have been the institutional drivers of this economic globalization process.

The Bretton Woods twins, the World Bank, and the IMF used the global debt crisis to discipline the Third World and to weaken the capabilities of Third World governments in dealing with Northern states, corporations and Northern dominated multilateral agencies. The World Bank's "structural adjustment" lending approach has been the key vehicle for the market liberalization program that was applied across the board to Third World economies.

Almost invariably, structural adjustment programs have the following elements:

• Radically reduce government spending on health, education and welfare

• Privatize and deregulate state enterprises

• Devalue the currency

• Liberalize imports and remove restrictions on foreign investment

• Cut or constrain wages and eliminate or weaken mechanisms protecting labor

By the late 1980s, with over 70 countries submitting to IMF and World Bank programs—structural adjustment and shock therapy—became the common condition of the South. Structural adjustment and related free market policies have been the central factor that globally triggered a sharp rise in inequality. A UN Conference on

Trade and Development study covering 124 countries showed that the income share of the richest 20 percent of the world's population rose from 60 percent to 83 percent between 1965 and 1990. Structural adjustment has also been a central cause of the lack of any progress in the campaign against poverty. The number of people living in poverty around the world- that is, on less than one U.S. dollar a day- increased from 1.1 billion in 1985 to 1.3 billion in 2000. A World Bank study has also confirmed that the absolute number of people living in poverty rose in the1990s in Eastern Europe, South Asia, Latin America and the Caribbean, and sub-Saharan Africa– all areas that came under the sway of adjustment programs—while the Bank's PR machine continues to chant its vision of a world without poverty!

STRATEGY FOR CHANGE

Today the tattered legitimacy of these international financial institutions requires that they hold their meetings under heavy police protection, whether in Genoa, Italy or in Washington, D.C.. The globalization from below now counterattacking corporate power has resulted in thousands of protestors joining forces in Seattle, Prague, Washington D.C., Davos, Gothenberg, Vancouver, Genoa, and elsewhere, creating a situation where these corporate dominated economic forces, can neither hide nor run. Thousands have celebrated the fact that there *is* a possibility of another world, one not shaped by closed-door meetings of profit-obsessed big business, as displayed at the annual World Social Forum in Porto Allegre..

It is against the dismal record of the World Bank and the IMF and the growing power of the social movement against them, that we have to address the question of what needs to be done.

All countries that are currently members of the WTO have existing human rights commitments and obligations under international treaties and conventions. These individual states, as well as the larger *community* of states, have an important regulatory role and responsibility to ensure that economic policies and practices do not undermine or conflict with human rights commitments. This is a legal mandate and not a mere policy option. However, these human rights obligations have not been taken into account while promoting the hegemony of the market.

The Universal Declaration of Human Rights (UDHR) guarantees a full range of economic human rights including the right to an adequate standard of living, which includes food, clothing, housing, medical care, necessary social services, etc. Yet the crisis caused by the policies of the World Bank, the IMF and the WTO, shows how far the U.S. and other governments have fallen short of their commitments under the UDHR. The urgency to implement economic and social human rights has never been more acute.

The range of international human rights instruments that are relevant to international trade, finance, and investment policy and practice is extensive. The starting point is the Charter of the United Nations. Article 5, which stipulates that the United Nations will promote higher standards of living, full employment, and conditions of economic and social progress and development, as well as "...universal respect for, and observance of human rights and fundamental freedoms for all..."

The International Bill of Rights (comprising the Universal Declaration of Human Rights (UDHR), the International Covenant on Civil and Political Rights (ICCPR) and the International Covenant on Economic, Social, and Cultural Rights (ICESCR), also contain vital provisions. In addition, there is the Declaration on the Right to Development, the Convention on the Elimination of All Forms of Discrimination against Women, the Convention on the Rights of the Child, the Charter of Economic Rights and Duties of States, the International Convention on the Elimination of Racial Discrimination, several conventions promulgated by the International Labor Organization (ILO), the declarations of several world conferences (including those held in Rio de Janiero, Copenhagen, Cairo, Beijing Istanbul, and Rome) and a host of regional instruments.

Those engaged in the process of international economic policy formulation invariably seek to erect a "firewall" between economic policy and social or human rights policy. They claim that these matters are logically and practically separate, and that economic policy processes should not be burdened with "social" considerations. The growing social movement against this economic warfare will have to tear down that artificial firewall in order to build another world based on the principles of justice and fairness. The foundation for this international movement will based on the following arguments:

KEVIN DANAHER

• Fundamental rights and freedoms set out in human rights treaties and conventions are an internationally agreed upon set of norms and standards, and essential for human dignity and well-being.

• These rights and freedoms have the status of international law and are binding upon states.

• The promotion and protection of human rights is (as declared by the vast majority of nation states at the 1993 World Conference on Human Rights) the first responsibility of governments, and cannot be subordinated to other priorities.

• Economic policy which benefits a small minority at the expense of the majority is contrary to the principles of human rights and fundamental freedoms.

• Policies and practices of international financial institutions need to be constantly tested against, and guided by, the legal obligations contained in the international human rights instruments.

This international human rights agenda presents a valuable approach that can strengthen civil society efforts that are challenging the global economic regime.

In *10 Reasons to Abolish the IMF and the World Bank*, Kevin Danaher, one of the leading and most passionate voices in the international movement for social and economic justice, shatters the lies promulgated by the international financial institutions to establish the supremacy of the market over people's lives. He cogently outlines how trade liberalization is not redistributing wealth to non-industrialized countries, but in fact further widening the huge gap between the rich and poor in all nations. He reveals how the lending policies of the IMF and the World Bank do not provide development aid to the Third World, as they would have us believe, but line the pockets of dictators and western corporations while threatening local democracies and forcing cuts to social programs.

Taking the reader inside people's lives, Danaher calls out to abolish the World Bank and the IMF, asserting:

We abolished slavery; we abolished Jim Crow laws, we abolished child labor, we abolished the exclusion of women from voting, we abolished the 60-hour work week, and we can abolish international banking institutions that do more to *prevent* democracy than to promote it.

The goal of the people's movement is to reframe the basic terms on which international economic policies are formulated, using the principles of human rights. Only then will it be possible for a fair and just world for all!

The message is clear: trade agreements must be first and foremost tested in economic human rights terms, not just in narrow economic criteria which benefit the few. Fortunately, there is an existing and overarching framework of legal principles and commitments against which those policies and agreements can and must be tested — the body of international human rights law. It is time for workers, activists, peasants, and landless workers movements of the world to unite!

INTRODUCTION

In 1984 my wife, Medea Benjamin, and I were conducting research interviews with Guatemalan peasant women whose husbands had been killed by the Guatemalan military. One of these women told us a story more illuminating than any lecture I had heard during my years in graduate school. She stood in front of her humble home, with her three beautiful children standing next to her, and told us how one night a Guatemalan military unit had come, dragged her husband from their home and hacked him to death with machetes, right in front of her and the children.

I asked, "Why did they do this?" She looked down at her hands, and replied, "They said he was a *subversivo* (a rebel)." I asked, "What was your husband doing that caused the military to label him subversive?" She answered, "He was a delegate of the word, a lay missionary. He was teaching other peasants how to raise rabbits."

I couldn't understand how helping other peasants raise rabbits makes you a threat to the system. I asked her to explain. She said, "You have to understand the structure of the society and the rules of power here. The structure of our economy in Guatemala is that the people in power, many of them generals, own and run the big plantations down in the lowlands, exporting things like cotton and fruit to you people in the United States.

The big landowners make a lot of money. They make big profits because they have people like us, peasants from the highlands, who are so desperately poor that we are forced by our poverty to go down to those plantations and endure that horrible work in the fields and get pesticides sprayed on us—all for just a dollar a day—because we have no alternative. So if we do things like teaching each other how to raise rabbits so we can feed ourselves without being forced to go and sell our labor for a dollar a day, that *is* subversive, given the structure of this system."

It was a lesson within a lesson. One of the lowest-income people on the planet was teaching the college-educated northerners a crucial lesson: it is the rich, not the poor, who create poverty.

So if we really want to get at the roots that cause poverty—not just its surface manifestations—we must commit ourselves to a larger and more long-term struggle than simply handing out relief supplies. You can rescue every drowning child out of the river, but if you don't go upstream to stop the guy who's throwing the kids in the water in the first place, you'll never get a real solution. You're going to suffer from "compassion fatigue," trying to save each victim *after* they have been victimized and not getting at the root causes of the problem.

It was people like this Guatemalan woman who gave us the insights that inspired us to establish Global Exchange in 1988, promoting what we call grassroots internationalism, and what some people call democratic globalization: linking people around the world who are struggling for economic justice and full democracy. This alternative to top-down globalization is founded on a simple (but not simplistic) idea: by bringing people together across national, racial, and cultural barriers, we can build a world of peace and prosperity for *all* the world's people.

When I first went to South Africa in the 1980s, wanting to assist the struggle against white minority rule, local activists told me some variant on this theme: "It's nice that you come here wanting to help us, but if you really want to help us, go back and change your country. It is your corporate and government leaders who are supporting undemocratic leaders all over the world. Your best contribution would be to sever the links of solidarity between your élites and our élites, while building solidarity among grassroots forces."

Most of the work of the global justice movement seeks to build direct links between grassroots movements here and our counterparts in countries around the world, while trying to expose and disrupt the unity of the transnational élite alliance. Whether it involves taking people from this country to visit grassroots struggles in other countries, bringing community leaders from the global south on speaking tours in the U.S., selling fair trade goods produced by poor people's organizations, mobilizing people to challenge corporate rule, or exposing the secret global government of the World Trade Organization (WTO), the World Bank, and the International Monetary Fund (IMF), we have relied on a matchmaker's calculation: if you bring people together in a context where they feel safe, they will interact, change each other, and move toward redefining love from an individualistic vision that sees relationships as private islands of happiness in a sea of misery, to a more planetary vision that sees all people as brothers and sisters.

This book seeks to get at the root causes of three major problems afflicting our planet: social injustice, environmental destruction, and moral bankruptcy. Only by understanding the dominant worldview of wealthy policy makers can we find a solution to these huge problems. Although the book focuses on two of the most powerful institutions shaping the direction of the global economy (the World Bank and the IMF), it is also a larger critique of the values and rules promoted by those institutions, and the large corporations which are the main beneficiaries of the free market dogma.

Stagnation in the global economy and the mounting protests against corporate globalization have produced an ideological crisis among corporate and government leaders. On November 30, 1999 in Seattle, 50,000 protesters made history by preventing the World Trade Organization from launching a new round of corporate-driven rule making for the planet. Never before had an international trade ministers conference broken down so completely that it failed to issue even a final communiqué. Élites around the world were so intimidated by the mass street protests that the WTO could find only one country willing to host the next big conference: the tiny Middle Eastern kingdom of Qatar. Yet there will be massive protests around the world during those days (November 9-13, 2001) to show the rule makers that we *will* be heard no matter where they hide.

Tens of thousands of well-organized, militant protesters transformed the annual meetings of the World Bank and International Monetary Fund from an abstract event that would have been ignored by the mass media to visceral protests that brought international media attention to public outrage over of globalization and it's threat to labor, the environment, and democracy.

The annual meetings of the G-8 industrial country leaders also attract growing protest action. Hundreds of thousands of people took to the streets of Genoa, Italy, in July 2001. The Italian government resorted to widespread police violence in an attempt to silence criticism of G-8 polices regarding issues such as third world debt, the environment, and immigration rights.

The increasing public pressure on the ruling institutions of the global economy have caused fractures within the élite classes. There hasn't been this much lack of consensus regarding the rules of the global economy since the end of World War II when current rule-making institutions such as the World Bank and the IMF were created. A special report ("Global Capitalism") in the November 6, 2000 issue of *Business Week* admitted that the growing protests against corporate globalization "have helped to kick-start a profound rethinking about globalization."

Now it's time to get realistic. The plain truth is that market liberalization by itself does not lift all boats, and in some cases, it has caused severe damage. What's more, there's no point denying that multinationals have contributed to labor, environmental, and human-rights abuses.[1]

Whereas most of the proposals in the mainstream press call for tinkering with the current rules of the game (trying to mitigate the worst effects of rapid transnational capital flows), the movement for grassroots globalization argues for a deeper critique of the fundamental workings of the global market economy.

A key argument of the global justice movement is that if we are to have real democracy, then sovereignty ("supreme political authority" —*Webster's Unabridged*) must reside in the people themselves, not in institutions with limited public accountability such as corporations. Yet the globalization of market forces has raised transnational corporations to a status where they—not the people—have the most power over society and the environment.

Two of the most powerful institutions that have promoted the "free market" agenda of the large corporations are the World Bank and the IMF. By lending hundreds of billions of dollars to third world élites, the World Bank and the IMF exert significant control over the economic strategy of most countries. They have promoted a set of policies ("structural adjustment"[2]) and an economic model that greatly benefit a minority and harm the majority.

Despite the disastrous results of World Bank/IMF policies, third world élites continue to implement them because they are on a treadmill of debt. If they implement corporate-friendly policies, they get more money; if they focus on pleasing their own population rather than transnational corporate managers, they get isolated in the international capital markets. So poor countries continue to take on more debt and implement policies focused on exporting into a world market skewed in favor of large corporations.

This is why the mountain of debt carried on the backs of the world's poor continues to grow. In six of the eight "boom" years from 1990 to 1997, developing countries

KEVIN DANAHER

paid more in debt service (interest plus principle repayments) than they received in new loans.[3]

Debt payments have become such an intolerable burden for many countries that the IMF, the World Bank, and many industrial country governments have been forced to offer debt "relief." The notorious Highly Indebted Poor Countries (HIPC) Initiative initially made great promises but failed to deliver significant change in the treadmill of debt.

Cameroon, for example, will have its annual debt payments reduced by 40 percent over the next five years, but the country will still be paying an average of $280 million per year, compared to $239 million per year spent on education and $87 million per year spent on health care.[4] How can we justify a poor country giving more money each year to wealthy bankers than it spends educating its children or healing its sick?

Unless we break this treadmill of debt (along with the policy conditions attached to new loans), the economic and ecological crises afflicting poor countries will continue to worsen.

This book presents ten arguments for abolishing the World Bank and the IMF and replacing them with democratic institutions that would make the global economy more accountable to an informed and active citizenry. It may sound extreme at first, but abolition has a solid history in many societies. We abolished slavery; we abolished Jim Crow laws, we abolished child labor, we abolished the exclusion of women from voting, we abolished the 60-hour work week, and we can abolish international banking institutions that do more to *prevent* democracy than to promote it.

While it is not the place for any one person to construct a blueprint of the institutions that could replace the World Bank and the IMF, in Chapter 10 and the Conclusion to this book we review grassroots movements and democratic principles that will play an important role in replacing the World Bank and the IMF.

A key assumption of the movement is that a democratic global economy *will* some day exist: the question is, will that take 150 years or 15 years? The survival of human society as we know it hangs on the answer to that question.

NOTES

1. Special Report, "Global Capitalism: Can it be made to work better?" *Business Week*, November 6, 2000, p. 74.

2. Structural adjustment refers to a package of policies cooked up in Washington and Wall Street and imposed on third world debtor governments as a condition for receiving more loans. The main function of structural adjustment policies is to keep national economies open to penetration by transnational capital.

3. Wayne Ellwood, *The No-Nonsense Guide to Globalization*, (London: Verso, 2001), p. 47.

4. Rick Rowden, "A World of Debt: Why "Debt Relief" Has Failed to Liberate Poor Countries," *The American Prospect*, July 2-16, 2001, p. 31.

1

Markets Create Inequality

The globalization of market forces—vigorously promoted by the World Bank and the International Monetary Fund (IMF)—creates greater inequality.

Extensive data shows that inequality, both among nations and within nations, has been getting worse. The United Nations Development Program (UNDP) reports that the richest 20 percent of the world's population consume 86 percent of the world's resources, and the poorest 80 percent consume just 14 percent of the world's resources.[1] Global inequality today is far more extreme than anything that existed at the end of World War II, when the IMF and the World Bank were created.

This severe global inequality results in a child dying from hunger on an average of one every few seconds. Children are dying from malnutrition-related diseases. They are dying from diseases such as measles, the vaccine for which costs mere pennies. They are dying at a rate of one every ten seconds from drinking polluted water (the "cure" consisting of clean water with a bit of sugar and salt). Imagine the agony of the parents of these children who are forced to watch their children suffer and die, knowing that there is abundance in the world.

Millions of people suffer like this because nearly all goods and services in the global economy are distributed via market mechanisms. For example, well over 90 percent of all the grain shipments in the world are commercial transactions; only a small amount comes in the form of humanitarian aid.

Markets are driven by money, or "effective demand." In a market economy you only get things if you have the money to pay for them. If your mind is challenged to think of any other way to do it, just think of your local public library: it's a "socialist" institution. Money is not the dominant factor connecting people to books in a library; rather, it is the right of all people to gain access to knowledge. Why shouldn't that principle of human rights be extended to other necessary goods and services such as food, housing, and health care?

Markets also tend to concentrate more and more wealth in fewer and fewer hands. As the wealthy minority gets richer and more powerful, they are increasingly able to acquire more of the property owned by weaker sectors of the population. Globalization of markets makes this tendency worse because the larger a market becomes, the more it favors the biggest players who are best able to take advantage of growing economies of scale. Relying on market forces means consigning billions of people to a degrading life of suffering and injustice.

Was there always such extreme global inequality? Of course not! Go back 500 years to the beginning of the global market economy. There was *localized* inequality but there was *not* significant global inequality. Centuries ago a tribal chief in Africa might consume more food and other resources than the average villager, but widespread famines did not occur until after European colonizers forced Africans to put their best farmland and labor into export crops destined for foreign markets.

Compare the standard of living in Europe, from whence Christopher Columbus came, to the standard of living of peoples in Africa, Asia, and Latin America. Who had the higher standard of living in terms of real quality of life? In Europe, they had plagues wiping out millions of people, they had the Inquisition in which people were getting their kneecaps smashed with hammers to get them to admit that they were possessed by the devil. Thousands of women were burned at the stake as "witches," mainly for the "crime" of practicing midwifery and folk medicine. The same King Ferdinand and Queen Isabella of Spain who financed Columbus also violently expelled from the Iberian peninsula some 170,000 Jews who refused to convert to Catholicism.

Now look at the people living where Columbus landed in the Caribbean. Columbus' own diary reports that Native Americans such as the Arawaks, Tainos, and Caribes enjoyed a far more "civilized" life-style than any society in Europe: the natives only worked the equivalent of a few days per week, pulling fish from the sea and taking fruit from the trees; their children often accompanied them during work and they made a game of it; they displayed no shame, wearing little or no clothing; they had no guilt, making love openly; and they were so generous that anything the Europeans showed interest in was promptly given to them. The reader of Columbus' diary expects Columbus to then say, "we should send our best scholars to study these people and learn from them." Instead, Columbus writes:

"They do not bear arms, and do not know them, for

I showed them a sword, they took it by the edge and cut themselves out of ignorance. They have no iron. Their spears are made of cane... They would make fine servants... With fifty men we could subjugate them all and make them do whatever we want."[2]

Then Columbus and the other European conquerors touched off one of the worst cases of genocide in world history: tens of millions of Native Americans would die from the direct and indirect impacts of the European conquest.

What was driving Columbus? He and the other conquerors were looking for gold and silver, that is, money! What drove the major colonial powers to violently subjugate most of Africa, Asia, and Latin America? What drove the slave trade? What drove the colonizers of America to exterminate the Native Americans? What drove all the violent acquisition of wealth that formed the foundation of today's global market economy? It was money and power, which are very seldom separated because either money buys power or power seizes wealth.

None of this is to say that there was no injustice or inequality in pre-conquest societies. The Mayan, Aztec, and other civilizations conquered neighboring people, used systems of forced labor, and exhibited other cultural traits we would find unacceptable today. But this was local and regional injustice. The system of *global* inequality began five centuries ago when sailing ships mounted with cannons left Europe and proceeded to forcibly integrate other parts of the planet into the first truly global economic system: a system obsessed by money.

KEVIN DANAHER

RACE AND CLASS

The 500-year history of global capitalism has left us with a legacy of structural racism. The people who conquered the world tended to be white and the people being conquered were other than white. This made it easier for the conquering classes to assign "other" status to those conquered, justifying their brutality with an assortment of ideological rationales: the conquered people were savages; they were inferior and didn't deserve humane treatment; they were being brought to Christ and salvation; and many others.

Through centuries of justifying the violent redistribution of wealth on a global scale (from Africa, Asia, the Middle East and Latin America to Europe and North America), a massive edifice of institutionalized racism was constructed. There is no way we can seriously address this legacy of racism without confronting the structural inequalities that evolved hand-in-glove with the ideology of racial inferiority/superiority. To implement the concept "eracism" (the eradication of the notion that any one group of people is inherently superior to any other) we *must* restructure the extreme inequality that currently afflicts the human race. This massive redistribution of wealth on a global scale will *not* be achieved by banking institutions that place profit over people, and specialize in transferring wealth from the many to the few.

IT'S IN YOUR BACK YARD

Inequality is also severe and getting worse within the United States. Charts 1 and 2 on the next page show that

GRAPH 1

Distribution of Stock Ownership in the United States, 2000

Poorest 95% Percent of Stock Owners Own 18.1%

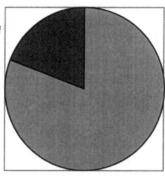

Richest 5% of Stock Owners Own 81.9%

GRAPH 2

Distribution of Net Worth in the United States, 2000

Poorest 95% of Americans Own 42.6%

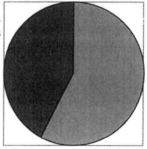

Richest 5% of Americans Own 57.4%

Source: James Poterba, "Stock Market Wealth and Consumption," *Journal of Economic Perspective*, Vol. 14, #2, Spring 2000.

GRAPH 3

Pay for Top U.S. Corporate Executives As a
Percentage of Average Worker Pay

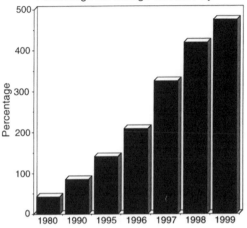

Source: *Business Week* special issue on
executive compensation, multiple years.

the richest 5 percent of the U.S. population owns 81.9
percent of corporate stock, and controls 57.4 percent of
the net worth of all people in the United States. Obvi-
ously, such concentration of wealth makes real democracy—equal access to power—impossible.

The conservative *Economist* magazine reports in its
January 16, 1999 issue that: "Whereas the average earn-
ings of the top fifth of [U.S.] male earners rose by 4 percent between 1979 and 1996, those of the bottom fifth
fell by 44 percent."

As Graph 3 shows, back in 1980, the average chief
executive officer of a large U.S. corporation earned 42
times that of the average U.S. worker. By 1999, market-
driven growth had raised that inequality to a point

where the average CEO was making 475 times what the average worker earned. This casts more than a small amount of doubt on the argument that economic "growth" raises all (or even most) boats.

The reason for the growing inequality here and around the world is straightforward. Markets favor those with money, giving them opportunities to make even more money by taking it away from those with less wealth and less access to the rule-makers in government. The maxim, "the rich get richer and the poor get poorer," is not just a cliche, it is a fact. Property ownership has been getting more and more concentrated.

When people say, "let the market rule," they are really saying "let money rule" or, more accurately, "let those who control most of the money rule." If the distribution of joy and suffering are governed by market forces there will be increasing inequality for the simple reason that markets distribute goods toward those with more money and away from those with less money.

NOTES

1. United Nations Development Program, *World Development Report, 1998* (New York: Oxford University Press, 1998). On the reproduction of global poverty, see Belinda Coote, *The Trade Trap: Poverty and the Global Commodity Markets* (Oxford, UK: Oxfam, 1996). For detailed data on inequality in the United States, see Lawrence Mishel, et al., *The State of Working America, 2000/2001* (New York: Economic Policy Institute, 2001).

2. Christopher Columbus, *The Journals of the First Voyage*, edited and translated by B.W. Ife (Warminster, England: Aris and Phillips, 1990), October entry.

2

Growth: The Ideology of the Cancer Cell

Capitalism is the extraordinary belief that the nastiest of men, for the nastiest of reasons, will somehow work for the benefit of us all.
—JOHN MAYNARD KEYNES

Contrary to what the economists at the World Bank and the IMF have been preaching, no amount of market-driven "growth" will solve the key problems we face.

Just think of how often you have heard people justify the ideology of economic growth by saying, "A rising tide floats all boats." But for those who don't own boats or those whose boats have holes in them (the global majority), a rising tide only increases the gap between them and the wealthy minority.

In fact, market-driven "growth" is making things worse. Look at a period of rapid economic growth such as 1960 to the present. During that period the global economy experienced rapid growth in all the major indicators: production, foreign direct investment, international trade, international debt. Did inequality in the world get better or worse during that period? It got far worse. Did environmental destruction get better or worse during that period? It got far worse. Did our sense of community and spirituality get better or worse? Most would agree that these key indicators of quality of life have gotten worse.

"GROSS" NATIONAL PRODUCT?

Think about the way we measure economic growth: the annual percentage increase in Gross National Product (GNP). GNP counts all goods and services—no matter how destructive—as positive numbers.

For example, let's say I go into a bar and drink ten beers. All the money I spend on that beer is a positive contribution to GNP. Now I'm drunk. I drive away in my car, and I crash into a family in their car. They're all maimed, and require intensive medical care for the rest of their lives. The tow truck, the emergency crews, the court costs, any jail time I get sentenced to, and the lifetime of medical care for the victims are all positive additions to GNP.

If we were using sane social and environmental criteria, the effects of behavior such as drunk driving, cigarette smoking, toxic waste dumping, and pollution's impact on public health would be *negative* numbers subtracted from GNP, not positive numbers as they are now.

The nonprofit group Redefining Progress has developed a statistical indicator called the Genuine Progress Indicator (GPI) that does precisely this. By subtracting from the value of production the costs of cleaning up toxic waste dumps, reclaiming polluted rivers, mending people maimed by the industrial system, the GPI better reflects the real, sustainable growth of the economy. Graph 4 shows that when they calculate the entire U.S.

economy using this more sensible measure—subtracting destruction from production—they find that the U.S. economy stopped growing in the 1970s and has been steadily declining since then.[1]

GRAPH 4

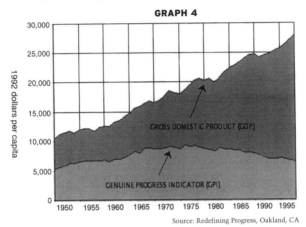

Source: Redefining Progress, Oakland, CA

By relying on the narrow economic criteria of the market to measure growth, we are systematically deceived about the underlying destruction being wrought by the global market economy.[2]

Look at the how we have been deceived about the "efficiency" of the market economy. If you ask Americans if U.S. agriculture is efficient, the majority will give a resounding yes as their answer. But consider the way that alleged efficiency is measured. The social and environmental costs of U.S. agriculture are excluded from the calculation of efficiency. The fact that agriculture is the primary source of water pollution in the United States does not get factored into the equation.

The destruction of beneficial insects by chemical-intensive farming is not factored into the equation. The value of the billions of tons of topsoil lost from U.S. farms every year is not factored into the equation. The bankrupting of family farmers whose land gets gobbled up by corporate agribusiness is not factored into the equation. In sum, if we measured our food system's productivity broadly—including all social and environmental costs—rather than just in narrow money terms, we would see that our food system is highly inefficient.

So the growth ideology must be challenged. The one thing in nature that has an ideology of unregulated growth is the cancer cell that propels a malignant tumor. The uniqueness of the cancer cell is that it has an "on" switch with no "off" switch. What does a malignant tumor do to its biological host? It kills it. What is the global market economy doing to its biological host—the earth's air, water, and soil? It is killing them. The "off" switch, or social immune system, for the cancer of global capitalism is we the people.

The World Bank and the IMF are the two most powerful enforcers of the growth ideology and a system of measurement that hides the social and environmental costs of market-led growth. Without major changes in these institutions, there is little hope that we will be able to convert to a more sane way of measuring economic progress.

NOTES

1. The Genuine Progress Indicator (GPI) was developed by the Oakland, California group Redefining Progress (510) 444-3041. The GPI subtracts from the value of total production the costs of things such as the health effects of tobacco consumption, cleaning up toxic waste from factories, and other costs to society that are currently counted as positive figures in standard GNP and GDP accounting.

2. See Chapter 21 of Kevin Danaher, ed., *Corporations Are Gonna Get Your Mama : Globalization and the Downsizing of the American Dream* (Monroe, ME: Common Courage Press, 1996); Herman E. Daly & John B. Cobb, Jr., *For the Common Good: Redirecting the Economy Toward Community, the Environment, and a Sustainable Future* (Boston: Beacon Press, 1989); Herman E. Daly, *Beyond Growth: The Economics of Sustainable Development* (Boston: Beacon Press, 1996).

3

Markets vs. Democracy

The dominant institutions of the global market economy—the World Bank, the International Monetary Fund, and the transnational corporations they represent—are not democratic either in terms of their internal functioning or in terms of the impact of their policies.

The major institutions that dominate the global market economy are autocracies: they are very hierarchical, and very elitist. The top executives have immense power over the lives of workers, customers, small businesses, and whole communities. Their public relations departments may talk about democracy but these institutions do not function in a democratic manner and they do not promote democratic practices. The historical record shows that they tend to weaken or destroy democratic social organizations such as trade unions, peasant groups, and other civic organizations.

The World Bank and the International Monetary Fund were created as specialized agencies of the United Nations. According to the UN Charter, these financial institutions were supposed to be under the control of the Economic and Social Council (ECOSOC) which is under the control of the UN General Assembly. This arrangement, had it been preserved, would have made the World Bank and IMF somewhat accountable to a broader constituency than just first-world banking interests. But note that the World Bank and IMF do *not* operate under the control of the General Assembly.

Not only are the officials running these powerful institutions unaccountable to the citizenry, the average citizen has no idea what the IMF and World Bank do. You can verify this by conducting an informal survey: Ask friends, family, or people on the street if they can give you one coherent sentence about the World Bank or IMF, and see what results you get.

Of course, the multilateral lending agencies spend huge sums on slick propaganda that portray their work as representing some generalized interest of what is best for "economic development." In recent years, as the World Bank and the IMF have come under more criticism, they have escalated their rhetoric about poverty and the environment. Hundreds of academics and NGOs who have examined the record of these institutions have seen that they represent the interests of the transnational corporations and banks that provide the IMF and World Bank with most of their capital and in turn get most of the contracts for "development" projects.[1]

The salaries of the Ph.D. economists at the World Bank and the IMF are so high that they earn more money in a few hours than most of the world's poor earn all year. It would be laughable, were the consequences not so tragic, to suppose that these privileged people could devise policies that would reverse the trend toward greater inequality.

The people making policies at the multilateral development banks create their plans in consultation with first world bankers and third world élites: they are so insulated from the poor majority that their policies usually do more to *reinforce* poverty than to alleviate it. Placing large sums of money in the hands of local élites better equips these ruling minorities to hang on to power and resist social pressure for change.

The very structure of power inside the IMF and the World Bank flies in the face of democratic principles. No less an authority than former Chief Economist at the World Bank, Joseph Stiglitz, points out the inherently undemocratic nature of the World Bank and the IMF:

The fundamental problem I see at the IMF and the World Bank is that the voting rights are not allocated on the principles of any democratic society. Most of the votes go to the wealthy industrial countries. In the United States and Europe no one would accept the principle that one dollar equals one vote. But this is the principle that underlies the IMF and the World Bank. The more money you have, the more votes you have.[2]

A key principle underlying all the work of the IMF and the World Bank is to get private corporations to invest in third world countries, assuming that this will automatically result in "development." Yet the fundamental aim of corporations is to make profits for their shareholders, not to foster development or democracy in the poor areas of the world. A private investor (individual or corporate) makes investments in another country for one central reason: in order to take out more than was put in. This is why corporations have never had many qualms about working hand-in-glove with dictators such as Marcos in the Philippines, Mobutu in Zaire, the Duvaliers in Haiti, the Shah of Iran, Pinochet in Chile, Suharto in Indonesia, the Saudi royal family, the white minority regime under apartheid in South Africa, the generals in Guatemala, the generals in Argentina, the generals in Brazil, the Communist Party in China, and a host of other antidemocratic enforcers of commercialism and profitability. The promoters of the "free market" never had any problem with dictators who butchered their own people, just so long as the butchers were willing to allow transnational corporations to penetrate national economies and tap the human and natural wealth.

CORPORATIONS SUBVERTING DEMOCRACY

Because the United States is the most powerful member of the IMF and the World Bank, it is important to understand how the pro-corporate agenda came to dominate U.S. policy making.

Early in America's history corporations were created through special government-issued charters that strictly limited what a corporation could do, how it could invest its capital, and how long it could exist. There were explicit requirements that corporations must serve the public interest. Indeed, serving the public interest was the fundamental reason for the very existence of corporations. State governments had the right, and exercised it regularly during the early 1800s, to revoke the charters of corporations in violation of the public trust.[3]

American democracy was founded on the radical concept that sovereignty resides in the people themselves, not in any institution. The fourth branch of government—intended to rule over the other three—is the citizenry. We are supposed to be a "self-governing" people. When Abraham Lincoln concluded the Gettysburg address he did *not* refer to government "of the corporations, by the corporations, and for the corporations."

In the early days of the American Republic, when it became clear that corporations were growing in size and political power, Thomas Jefferson said: "I hope we shall crush in its birth the aristocracy of our moneyed corporations, which dare already to challenge our government to a trial of strength and bid defiance to the laws of our country."[4]

In 1864 Abraham Lincoln (the "father" of the Republican Party) warned of the growing power of corporations. He wrote:

I see in the near future a crisis approaching that unnerves me and causes me to tremble for the safety of my country. As a result of the war, corporations have been enthroned and an era of corruption in high places will follow, and the money power of the country will endeavor to prolong its reign until all wealth is aggregated in a few hands, and the Republic is destroyed. I feel at this moment more anxiety for the safety of my country than ever before, even in the midst of the war.[5]

Lincoln's fear of corporate power proved to be well-founded. As corporations grew in size and gained more political power, they were able to gradually replace the definition of a corporation as a *public* institution with the mythology that corporations are *private* contractual agreements among persons and they should (1) have the same legal status as individuals, and (2) only be accountable to the owners of the company. A key turning point came in the 1886 Supreme Court decision in the *Santa Clara County v. Southern Pacific Railroad* case which ruled that the corporation should enjoy the same constitutional guarantees to due process as those extended to all citizens by the 14th Amendment. Other landmark legal cases in the late 19th century solidified the transfer of human rights to the corporation by ruling that "the term 'person' in the due-process clause applied to artificial persons, i.e., corporations, as well as individuals."[6]

The weakening of state governments' ability to regulate the scope and behavior of the corporations allowed these fictional "persons" to expand across state borders, thus making it more difficult for state and local governments to control their economies. That same process has been replicated in recent decades on a grander scale as corporations have expanded across national borders and have steadily eroded the sovereignty of national governments.

While corporations shape nearly every detail of our daily lives—what we eat, how we work, how our children are raised, what we hold sacred, how our government makes policy—the average citizen feels powerless to affect the policies of large corporations. Can there be anything more undemocratic than citizens who believe they are helpless to change fundamental aspects of their society?

NOTES

1. See Kevin Danaher, Ed., *50 Years Is Enough: The Case Against the World Bank and the International Monetary Fund* (Boston: South End Press, 1995), and Kevin Danaher, ed.,

Democratizing the Global Economy: The Battle Against the World Bank and International Monetary Fund (Monroe, ME: Common Courage Press, 2001); Catherine Caufiled, *Masters of Illusion: The World Bank and the Poverty of Nations* (New York: Henry Holt and Company, 1996).

2. "Raising a Ruckus" documentary by KQED television San Francisco, 2001.

3. See Charles Derber, *Corporation Nation: How Corporations Are Taking Over Our Lives and What We Can Do About It* (New York: St. Martin's Press, 1998). Also see the extensive work by the Program on Corporations Law and Democracy (POCLAD), www.poclad.org, (800) 316-2739.

4. Thomas Jefferson to George Logan, 1816 (http://etext.lib.virginia.edu/jefferson/quotations).

5. President Abraham Lincoln, November 21, 1864 (letter to Col. William F. Elkins) in Archer H. Shaw, *The Lincoln Encyclopedia* (New York: Macmillan, 1950), p. 40.

6. Derber, *Corporation Nation*, p. 130.

4

Redefining Corruption

The most important function of élite, market ori-
ented institutions such as the World Bank and the IMF
is *political*, not economic. They create stronger alle-
giance and accountability between third world élites and
first world élites than exist between third world élites
and their own people.

Global economic policy is made through an institutional web of collaborations by élites, dominated by the
leaders of the major industrial countries. By providing
large loans to third world élites, the first world élites
who dominate the multilateral lending agencies and the
private corporations are able to shape third world economic policies. The overall thrust of these policies is
to keep the workers and natural resources of third world
countries open to exploitation by transnational corporations.

Think of how a typical infusion of capital from the
World Bank or IMF transpires. The well-paid officials of
the multilateral lending institutions meet with local
élites (mainly political leaders but also corporate officials and generals) and agree to lend huge amounts of
money if the local élites are willing to implement policies crafted in Washington and Wall Street. Typically
these policies call for: keeping your economy open to
foreign capital, allowing liberal repatriation of profits;
keeping wages, trade unions and environmental restric-

tions at a minimum; balancing the government's budget (often by cutting social services); and focusing economic strategy on exporting raw and semi-processed goods to the wealthy markets of the global north.

Details of the debt negotiations are kept secret until the contract is signed, thus preventing the citizens who will pay the debt from having any meaningful participation in the negotiations. After signing on the dotted line, the local élites have considerable leeway in how they will spend the money. That is why the third world is plagued by overspending on military and police (used more to keep unpopular élites in power than to protect against foreign enemies), and an abundance of "white elephant" projects that were managed by some dictator's son-in-law.

This is not to say that there are no disagreements between third world élites and their financiers in the north. But the occasional outburst by someone like Mahatir Mohammed of Malaysia, who in 1998 criticized global financial markets for swamping small countries like his, stands out because it is so rare.

The norm is for third world élites to take on more debt in order to continue making payments on previous debt, and then implement policies that are favorable to global corporations. The simple fact is this: first world élites and third world élites collaborate in extracting wealth from the majority population and transferring that wealth upward in the global class structure. That is why we have more and more billionaires (in both north and south) and more people falling into poverty (in both north and south).

We can visualize this "transnational élite alliance" as being similar to a rope. A rope is made up of many small threads twisted together. First world élites and third world élites are bound together by a myriad of trade deals, direct investments, interlocking boards of directors, treaties, loans, military hardware purchases, military training, cooperation agreements, membership in the same private clubs, ownership of stock in each other's companies, children attending the same private schools, intermarriage, and many other links.

These élite linkages can be diagrammed. In the drawing below each big triangle represents a nation, with the small triangles at the top representing the ruling élites. The lines connecting the élites of the two nations can be dissected, each representing a specific connection, such as a loan from the World Bank or IMF (complete with policy strings attached), a military agreement, a direct investment by a transnational corporation, a trade agreement, local élites sitting on the board of directors of a transnational corporation, training at élite U.S. universities for the children of third world leaders, and many more.

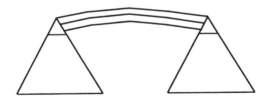

This web of institutional and personal ties binding the transnational élite alliance provides a more accurate way of examining power in the world than the analysis of "international relations" served up by the corporate media and most of academia. The daily press and the academic literature make the same mistake of analyzing global events using the nation-state as the main unit of analysis. For example, we read statements about the United States, Canada, and Mexico signing the North American Free Trade Agreement (NAFTA). But it was not the United States or Canada or Mexico that signed NAFTA, it was the ruling élites of those countries. The overwhelming majority of the citizens of those countries did not know (and still don't know) the details of NAFTA because the leaders made no effort to inform or engage the public on the issue. Positing the nation-state as a unified rational actor may make it easy to talk about global affairs but it is extremely misleading because it conceals the real central force at work: the transnational élite alliance.

One of the key functions of institutions such as the World Bank and the IMF is to maintain functional unity within the transnational alliance of élites. The banking institutions make huge loans to third world leaders in exchange for those leaders implementing policies that are favorable to first world banks and corporations. For example, the World Bank and IMF insist that attracting transnational capital is essential for any country to "develop" economically. In order to attract foreign capital, the debtor nation is advised to raise interest rates (the price paid to "rent" capital). These higher interest rates may inspire confidence at the big international

48

banks and they may purchase a government's bonds to take advantage of the higher interest rates, but what is the impact of high interest rates on the local economy? Small business people and working class consumers cannot afford to borrow at the higher interest rates, so the economy stagnates due to less mortgages, less car loans, and less borrowing for business expansion. Main Street is sacrificed for Wall Street.

The main problem with this arrangement is that policies written by wealthy outsiders will never end the inequality and the lack of democracy that plague most third world countries.

From this perspective, "corruption" is not a psychological phenomenon—a personality flaw of third world leaders—rather, it is a structural feature of the global political economy. The policy conditionally attached to each new loan puts third world economies under the control of outside élites, tempered by the political tastes and limited discretion of third world élites. As long as third world élites are more accountable to first world élites than to third world majority classes, there will never be real democracy or real development.

No amount of fine-tuning of aid or debt "relief" will liberate the third world majority unless third world élites become more accountable to their own people than they are to first world élites. This requires breaking the institutional linkages that currently bind third world élites to the policy prescriptions of first world élites. And that means replacing institutions such as the World Bank and IMF with institutions focused on building economic and cultural solidarity among majority classes rather than the wealthy.

This is the strongest argument for the abolition of institutions such as the World Bank and IMF. They serve primarily as a control mechanism for first world élites to shape economic policy in third world countries in such a way as to further the interests of transnational corporations and banks. That is why more than 50 years of policies produced by the transnational élite alliance have not solved the problems of inequality and environmental destruction.

5

Why No Success Story?

The comparative evidence from many different countries that have implemented the free market policies pushed by the World Bank and the IMF shows that these policies have been detrimental for the majority of people in those countries.

There is a parable about a villager who goes to a local wise man and asks to borrow the wise man's donkey. The wise man lies, saying his donkey is not there. Just then the donkey brays. There is a pregnant pause, and the wise man says: "Who are you going to believe, a wise man or a donkey?"

Despite massive evidence from dozens of countries that the "wise men" of the IMF and the World Bank have promoted policies that have hurt the majority, the "wise men" still insist that their free market prescriptions will work.

In my 1995 book, *50 Years Is Enough: The Case Against the World Bank and the International Monetary Fund,* various authors present evidence from thirteen countries showing a similar pattern: the structural adjustment policies attached to IMF/World Bank loans may help countries make payments on their old debts and may create some millionaires but the majority of the population suffers lower wages, reduced social services, and less democratic access to the policy making process.

Many of the most destitute countries—Somalia, Sudan, Zaire (now the Congo), Liberia, Rwanda—were for years under the influence of "structural adjustment" programs devised in Washington. The results in these countries have been disastrous: their economies are in worse shape now than they were thirty or forty years ago.

Yet even when we look at larger, more well-endowed third world countries—ones that are blessed with abundant natural resources—the results of structural adjustment are also bleak.

Brazil is a huge country with just about every natural resource you could imagine.[1] The country is a major producer of coffee, soybeans, corn, cocoa, sugar, oranges, animal products, wood, and a wide range of manufactured goods. The country's area of natural forest is greater than that of Canada and the U.S. combined. Yet despite Brazil's economic abundance, millions of Brazilians go hungry on a regular basis. The steady commercialization of agriculture has pushed tens of millions of family farmers off the land into crowded urban slums. There are between 7 million and 10 million abandoned children living on the streets with no adult supervision. Brazil ranks as one of the most unequal societies in the world. Although the government has been faithfully collaborating with IMF and World Bank officials in making payments on the foreign debt, Brazil is more deeply in debt now than it was twenty years ago. The end of the debt treadmill is nowhere in sight.

Mexico is well-endowed with petroleum, good farmland, abundant labor, mineral resources, forests, a rich coastline, and a good climate for tourism. Yet despite some years of high GDP growth rates, the standard of living of most Mexicans is worse now than it was twenty-five years ago. Since the 1994 inception of the North American Free Trade Agreement (NAFTA), the ordinary Mexican's purchasing power has decreased 39 percent and the number of people living in "severe" poverty (surviving on less than $2 a day) has increased by 4 million, according to the United Nations.[2] Fifty percent of the population is either unemployed or underemployed; the purchasing power of the minimum wage has fallen to less than what it was in the 1970s; family farmers are being forced off their farms by an influx of cheap U.S. corn and other crops ushered in by the free market policies of NAFTA; environmental destruction is mounting; poverty-driven crime has soared; and Mexico's foreign debt has grown.

Thailand had been following World Bank/IMF free market policies when the country was capsized in mid-1997 by the very global financial markets that Thai leaders were taught to defer to.

South Korea for decades had rejected a free market approach and prospered under state interventionist policies that directed investment to select industries, erected high tariff barriers to protect infant industries, and restricted capital flows and trading in the national currency. Several decades of these state interventionist policies (plus aid and trade assistance from the U.S. government, which wanted a successful capitalist counterpoint to North Korea's experiment with Stalinism) produced a rapid rise in the standard of living for most South Koreans. But in the 1990s—when the South Korean government was pressured by the World Bank, the IMF and the U.S. Treasury Department to open its financial markets—this successful economy was swamped by international short-term debt and speculative attacks on the South Korean currency. The resulting depression destroyed Korean lives and set the country back many years.

Across Africa there are dozens of countries that for decades have been under the tutelage of the free-market pushers, and what has it gotten them? Great amounts of wealth have been extracted from the continent, external debt has skyrocketed, real wages have declined, social services have deteriorated, the environment has been decimated, and hopelessness is spreading.

Whether you take the obvious "basket case" countries or the more well-endowed countries, free market policies concocted by extremely wealthy people in Washington and Wall Street simply do not have a record of creating real development for the majority population in third world countries.

We are not saying that *everything* wrong with these countries' economies has been due to the influence of the World Bank and the IMF. But wouldn't there be a *few* success stories if these free market economic policies were really sound?

NOTES

1. Michael Shellenberger and Kevin Danaher, eds., *Fighting for the Soul of Brazil* (New York: Monthly Review Press, 1995).

2. For detailed data showing the decline of the Mexican economy in recent years, see the pamphlet by Sarah Anderson, "Seven Years Under NAFTA" from the Institute for Policy Studies, Washington, D.C., (202) 234-9382, www.ips-DC.org. Also see the Public Citizen website www.tradewatch.org

6

Giving Hypocrisy a Bad Name

The industrial countries—both the G-8 countries[1] of the north and the newly industrializing countries such as Taiwan, Malaysia, China, and South Korea—did NOT develop by relying on a free market model.

While the World Bank and the IMF are coercing debtor country governments to adopt "free market" policies, there is a simple historical fact that has been ignored: All the countries that have successfully industrialized and raised the living standards of the broad majority have done it—*not* through a free market model—but through a state interventionist model, with government playing a strong role in directing investment, managing trade, and subsidizing chosen sectors of the economy.

All the industrialized countries of Europe, plus the newly industrialized countries of East Asia, used a wide range of government intervention to boost their economic development. The mythology promoted by the World Bank that free market policies were responsible for the industrialization of countries such as Taiwan and South Korea is simply false. These "success stories" in Asia, including Malaysia, Singapore, and, more recently China, achieved their relatively high economic growth rates through extensive state involvement in the economy.[2] These measures included land reform, tight control of trade, state enterprises, government-funded research and infrastructure, high tariff barriers to protect infant industries from foreign competition, and favoring certain sectors of the economy through subsidies and state-directed investment.

Look at South Korea, an economy that the free market promoters always point to as one of their success stories. Government was heavily involved in every stage of South Korea's recent economic development. Following the war of 1950-53, the U.S. government intervened in the shaping of the Korean economy and boosted its growth through aid and preferential trade access to the U.S. market for Korean goods. The Korean government used a range of programs to build up large corporate conglomerates called "chaebol," some of which are internationally powerful (e.g., Hyundai, Daewoo, Samsung). During the decades of the '50s, '60s, '70s, and '80s, the state interventionist policies raised South Korea's economy to a status equal to England and other industrial countries. It was during the late 1990s, when South Korea was pressured by Washington to open up its controlled economy to international market forces, that the economy crashed. Then the South Korean government was bailed out by another form of government, this time a multilateral agency (the IMF), but still using taxpayer money (a $58 billion loan) to rescue private capitalists from their excesses.[3]

So it is extremely misleading to portray any of the few success story countries as validating free market policies. Governments, using taxpayers' money to subsidize private corporations, have been heavily involved in shaping the direction of all the high-income economies. The key question is not about *whether* the government will be involved in the economy or not, but how it will be involved, in whose interest, and under whose control.

The United States was in many ways the "mother country" of protectionism, showing other countries how to do it. From its very inception as a nation, the United States used the federal government, as well as state and local governments, to assist corporations in a number of ways: defending them against foreign competition, developing a public education system, constructing ports, canals, railroads, electricity grids, the interstate highway system, and a wide range of other infrastructure, all of which made the U.S. economy a profitable arena for private capital.

Just think of the major U.S. industries that wouldn't exist in their present form had it not been for massive government subsidies (railroads, automobiles/highways/suburbia, computers, biotechnology). Would we have a big electronics industry or an avionics industry were it not for that massive government subsidy called the Pentagon? Would the nuclear power industry make any profits at all if it were forced to absorb the huge costs of disposing of nuclear waste without massive subsidies from the taxpayers?

It gives hypocrisy a bad name when the U.S. government and institutions it dominates such as the World Bank and the IMF go around the world pushing a free market model on third world countries when the historical record shows that neither the United States, nor any other wealthy country, used that model. Of course, it is not hypocrisy that drives the free market model; it is corporate power over policy making in Washington.

NOTES

1. The so-called G-8 (Group of 8) industrial countries are Japan, Canada, the United States, France, England, Germany, Italy, and Russia. Their leaders meet each year, usually in July, to plan economic strategy for the world even though their countries represent only about 13 percent of the global population.

2. See Walden Bello, *Dragons in Distress: Asia's Miracle Economies in Crisis* (Oakland, CA: Institute for Food and Development Policy, 1990).

3. For an insightful analysis of South Korea's development model, see Martin Hart-Landsberg, *Rush to Development* (New York: Monthly Review Press, 1993). For a detailed critique of how neoliberal economic policies contributed to the Asian economic crisis, see Paul Burkett and Martin Hart-Landsberg, *Development, Crisis, and Class Struggle: Learning from Japan and East Asia* (New York: St. Martin's Press, 2000).

7

The Market vs. Nature

The free market paradigm promoted by the IMF and the World Bank has been very destructive to the environment.

Markets are only capable of valuing things in terms of money. A tree has no value standing; it is only when the tree gets killed and turned into plywood and hot tubs that it generates market value. A fish swimming has no value; it is only when the fish is killed and marketed as a commodity that it generates value. Thus, destroying nature is genetic to the market economy. As long as destroying nature is profitable, and there are no countervailing social institutions powerful enough to stop the corporations, our biosphere *will* be trashed by the profit seekers.

Every biological system upon which human civilization rests is either in rapid decline or outright collapse. Topsoil is being destroyed by chemical-intensive and machine-intensive agriculture. Groundwater is being polluted and wasted at rates greater than what nature can replace. Some twenty-five million people (more than the world's refugee population) have been driven from their home communities by the spread of environmental destruction.[1] The glaciers are melting at rates much faster than the historical average. The polar icecaps are melting. Thousands of plant and animal species are being exterminated. The ozone layer that shields us and our crops from harmful levels of ultraviolet light is being eroded. Sea levels are rising due to global warming expanding the volume of the oceans. Extreme weather events are causing huge losses for people and property insurers.[2]

Go to third world fish markets where you haven't been in five or ten years and you see them selling tiny fish. You say: "Why are you selling such small fish?" They tell you: "Oh, the big fish are all gone." Or you see them selling bottom feeders that don't taste good and you ask: "Why are you selling these less palatable species?" They tell you: "The good-tasting fish are all gone." Look at the catch rates of cod, haddock, salmon, halibut, sturgeon, pilchards: they are all plummeting. They have been overfished at such a rate that it is destroying the ability of nature to reproduce these species.

When the World Bank and the IMF attach conditionality to their loans to debtor countries—"structural adjustment"—the central goal is for the debtor country to earn hard currency (dollars, pounds, marks, yen) in order to make payments on external debt. A key way to earn hard currency (other than direct investment or more loans) is to sell something in the global market. So, following the export-or-else mandate, if you have trees, cut them down; if you have farmland, throw chemicals on it to produce more export crops; if you have coastline or inland waterways, fish the hell out of them; if you have minerals in the ground, rip them out. The core of the strategy is "turn nature into dollars." And what do we see around the world as a result? There is a forestry crisis, a fisheries crisis, a soil depletion crisis, an air quality crisis, and a water quality crisis.[3]

In every major area of economic activity the World Bank has added to environmental destruction with the policies it has promoted. In the area of energy the World Bank promotes fossil fuels and nuclear power rather than renewable energy such as solar, wind, and geothermal. For decades the World Bank was the biggest promoter of large dams. These megaprojects proved extremely lucrative for transnational construction companies, but they displaced millions of poor people, destroyed large areas of farmland and forest, and channeled the electricity mainly to large enterprises running sweatshops and other export-oriented industries. In the area of transportation the World Bank promotes cars and highways rather than mass transit. In agriculture the World Bank has promoted chemical-intensive agriculture rather than organic agriculture. Their agricultural investments have promoted export agriculture focused on producing "dessert crops" for wealthy markets in the global north (coffee, tea, cocoa, bananas) rather than food crops for local people.

Notice that in each area the policies favored by the World Bank are lucrative for large corporations but not in the interest of local economies and the environment. Could this be related to the fact that large banks and corporate-owned politicians, especially in Washington, are the people with the most influence over World Bank policies?

Another neglected area of environmental destruction comes from trade. The greatest cause of species destruction is habitat destruction, but the second greatest cause of species destruction is international trade. Invasive species (Zebra mussel, kudzu vine, Asian tiger mosquito, giant African snail) ride on internationally traded goods and get introduced into bioregions with no predators for that species and the invasive species takes off, usually with costly results.[4]

Probably the most damaging area of the World Bank's impact on the environment has been its energy policies stressing fossil fuels rather than renewable sources. Roughly one-fifth of the World Bank's lending goes to the energy sector of third world countries, but the Bank spends about 25 times as much promoting fossil fuel development as it spends promoting renewable energy sources.[5] The World Bank does not even systematically report on the greenhouse gas emissions of the projects it funds. So much for the World Bank's claim to support "sustainable development."

Our planet's climate has been so disrupted by our massive output of carbon dioxide and other greenhouse gases that we are seeing a sharp increase in severe weather such as floods, droughts, and hurricanes. The Worldwatch Institute reports that property damage from weather-related disasters jumped from $3 billion in 1980 to $89 billion in 1998.

As Ross Gelbspan shows in his book, *The Heat Is On*, a major obstacle to accepting the reality of global climate destruction is that the fossil fuels industry can rent scientists capable of confusing the public debate—asserting that global warming is just a theory—in order to slow down the process of environmental regulation.[6] With hindsight, we know that this is precisely how the tobacco industry for decades threw doubt on the scientific evidence linking smoking to cancer. But that should not confuse us about the need to gain democratic control over economic planning and put a halt to the destruction of our natural life-support systems.

With all this blatant environmental destruction, have the World Bank and IMF taken the lead in calling for emergency action to save the biological systems that are now in a state of collapse? No they haven't. Why? Because getting at the causes of environmental destruction requires the recognition that there is a fundamental contradiction between the money cycle and the life cycle. You cannot promote a market-driven system that single-mindedly seeks to convert nature and human creativity into money, and not at the same time destroy nature. Because the World Bank and the IMF are dogmatically wedded to a free-market ideology, they are incapable of making the changes necessary to save the environment from destruction.

We can learn an important lesson from the early days of deep-pit coal mining. The miners, though they were relatively unschooled, knew enough to take canaries down into the mines with them because canaries are more sensitive to deadly gases that can build up in coal mines. When the canary would stop singing or slump into the bottom of its cage, the miners knew that they had better get out of the mine.

Nature is now presenting us with so many versions of the dying canary, we have no excuse for not realizing what is happening. To think that the environmental crisis is not directly related to the undemocratic way our global economy is run is fantasy of the most dangerous sort.

NOTES

1. See the website of the group World Overpopulation Awareness (www.overpopulation.org/impacts).

2. For documentation of these and other danger signs related to global climate change, see Ross Gelbspan, *The Heat Is On: The Climate Crisis, the Cover-up, the Prescription* (Redding, MA: Perseus Books, 1998).

3. Worldwatch Institute, *State of the World* 2000 (New York, NY: W.W. Norton, 2000); and Michael Goldman, ed., *Privatizing Nature: Political Struggles for the Global Commons* (London: Pluto Press, 1998).

4. The World Conservation Union (IUCN) has set up an Invasive Species Specialist Group (ISSG) comprising 146 scientific and policy experts on invasive species from 41 countries. See the website www.issg.org for a database of 100 invasive species.

5. Daphne Wysham, "The World Bank: Funding Climate Chaos," *The Ecologist*, March/April 1999. Also see Ken Hampton, "Smokescreen," *The New Internationalist*, December 1999. Check the excellent website of the Sustainable Energy and Environment Network (www.seen.org).

6. Gelbspan, *The Heat Is On*.

8

Downsizing the American Dream

So-called free market policies have been detrimental to the majority of people even in the richest, most powerful country: the United States.

At the end of World War II there was only one industrial country whose military and economic institutions were globally powerful—the United States. The political and economic space opened by the collapse of the European and Japanese colonial empires paved the way for U.S. corporations to move their production facilities to lower wage areas of the world. As more and more U.S. companies became transnational and began sourcing their materials and labor in other countries, a free market ideology was developed to give intellectual weight and popular appeal to policies that would make it easier for U.S. companies to behave in unpatriotic ways. This free market dogma—reduce democratic controls over capital—has come to dominate the official discourse.

The key goal of the free market agenda has remained hidden from the U.S. public. We have been told that it's all about trade: the names of key organizations and treaties feature the word trade prominently (North American Free *Trade* Agreement, World *Trade* Organization, Free *Trade* Area of the Americas). But the free market agenda had a central objective that had to be kept secret: shifting the tax burden from the large corporations to workers and the small business sector.

Although corporations steadily moved their production out of the United States to lower wage countries, they still wanted to sell the final products in the United States. When corporations move products or parts of products across borders they pay a special tax called a tariff. For corporations to increase the profitability of a transnational system of production they needed to lower the taxes (tariffs) they were paying. Hence the resurgence of free market ideology and policies. The first six rounds of trade negotiations under the GATT (General Agreement on Tariffs and Trade)— from 1947 to the 1970s—focused on lowering corporate taxes.

Ravi Batra's *The Pooring of America: Competition and the Myth of Free Trade,* shows convincingly that periods of rapid and broad-based industrialization in the United States coincided with high tariffs. Since the 1970s, when the U.S. started opening its markets, dropping tariff rates to historic lows, and loosening capital controls to allow U.S. capital to leave the country more easily, we have suffered the decimation of our manufacturing sector, declining average wages, growing inequality, an increase in the average work week, a ballooning deficit in the U.S. balance of trade, and a growing mountain of debt (government debt, consumer debt, corporate debt) necessary to keep the economy moving.

GRAPH 5

Average U.S. Tariff Rates, 1950-1995
(percent)

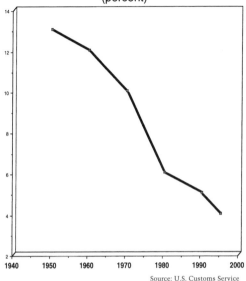

Source: U.S. Customs Service

Graph 5 shows how "tariffs" (i.e., taxes paid by transnational capital) have been pushed downward by U.S. policy makers during the post-World War II period. Taxes on globalized capital are given a code word—tariffs—so the public won't understand what is really going on. Another measure of this tax reduction on items produced abroad is the relationship between the value of U.S. imports and the value of taxes collected on those imports. Graph 6 on the following page shows that as imports flooded the U.S. market (much of it produced by U.S. corporations that had moved their factories abroad) the taxes collected on these imports by our government declined steeply.

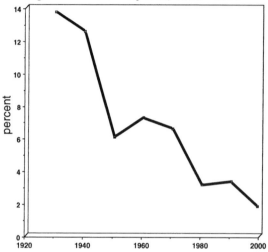

GRAPH 6

U.S. Import Taxes Collected as Percentage of Value of Imports, 1930 - 1999

Source: U.S. International Trade Commission,
*Value of U.S. Imports for Consumption, Duties
Collected, and Ratio of Duties to Values, 1891–1999.*

Tax changes are always redistributive: if you lower taxes in one sector of society, you must raise them in other sectors. Graph 7 shows that corporate taxes have declined relative to what families pay. Back in the 1950s, for every dollar paid in federal, state, and local taxes by families, corporations paid nearly 80 cents, but by the 1990s that had dropped to 21 cents.

KEVIN DANAHER

GRAPH 7

For Every One Dollar Paid by Families in Federal, State and Local Taxes, Corporations Have Paid a Declining Share

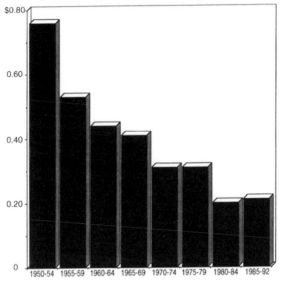

Source: Donald Bartlett and James Steele, *America: Who Really Pays the Taxes* (New York: Touchstone, 1994)

Graph 8 on the following page shows that while corporate income taxes have increased only slightly, individual income taxes have skyrocketed.

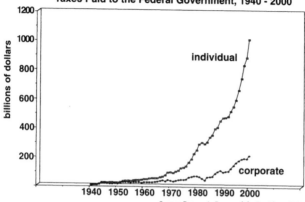

GRAPH 8
U.S. Corporate Income Taxes and Individual Income Taxes Paid to the Federal Government, 1940 - 2000

Source: Economic Report of the President, 2001.

Not all of the tax cuts on the corporate élites could be replaced by increased taxes on working class families: that might have touched off a rebellion. As Graph 9 shows, government policy makers made up the yawning budget deficit by issuing debt. During the Reagan administration alone the federal government accumulated more debt than during all previous administrations—from Washington through Carter—combined.

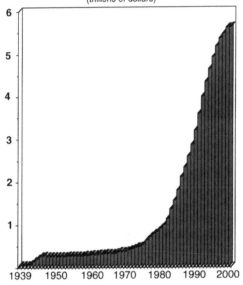

GRAPH 9
U.S. Federal Government Debt, 1939 - 2000
(trillions of dollars)

Source: Economic Report of the President, 2001.

Despite recent hype about budget surpluses, the interest payments on the accumulated federal debt has skyrocketed (see Graph 10, following page) to $400 billion per year. These interest payments are a massive transfer of wealth from American taxpayers to wealthy investors here and abroad who own trillions of dollars worth of U.S. government debt.

GRAPH 10

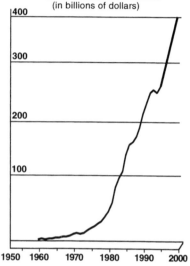

Annual Interest Payments on U.S. Federal Government Debt
(in billions of dollars)

Source: Economic Report of the President, 2000.

EMPIRE STIFLES DEMOCRACY

The impact of the free market agenda goes beyond the economy to the debasement of our political system at the hand of big money. Large corporations now dominate the funding of our political candidates. They employ high-paid lobbyists in Washington to ensure that they get to write the legislation that affects us all. They provide jobs to ex-government officials (the revolving door) so the companies are guaranteed access to government through the personal connections of former public servants. And they own the mass media which ensures that, instead of informing the citizenry about how the world actually operates, the main sources of information are focused on making money by selling consumers' minds to corporate advertisers. The result of all this is widespread ignorance about America's real role in the world.

Think about this huge paradox: the United States is the most potent global power ever in world history. Neither Rome, Greece, the Spanish empire, the Dutch empire, the British empire, the Japanese empire, nor any other, had the reach and power the United States has had since World War II. We would expect such a globally powerful nation to have citizens who are well-informed about global events. It's laughable on the face of it. Go around and ask average Americans basic questions about current global events and you will be astounded by the lack of information.

The only way to understand a globally powerful nation with citizens woefully ignorant of global affairs is to grasp that the dominant section of the U.S. ruling class is increasingly enmeshed in a *transnational* alliance of élites from many countries, collaborating to run the world in a way that redistributes wealth upward in the global class structure. The bankers and corporate lawyers running our country cannot go to the U.S. people and speak the truth by saying: "We have close and profitable ties with wealthy élites of other countries who allow our corporations to come into their countries and extract wealth, so we can't get too serious about labor rights or protecting the environment because that would lower our profits."

So instead of telling the truth, they concoct sophisticated policy rationales to make it sound as if the foreign policies they enact are in the "national interest" rather than mainly in the interests of large banks and transnational corporations.

The "free market" policies that have helped large corporations get even bigger have put increasing pressure on small business. In many sectors of the economy large corporations are pushing small entrepreneurs out of existence: family farms are being crushed by large agribusiness corporations; family-owned hardware stores are being eliminated by Home Depot and other large chain stores; independent bookstores have been decimated by Borders and Barnes and Noble. Critics of the neoliberal agenda are asking: Does free enterprise mean the freedom of large corporations to go anywhere and do anything they want, or does free enterprise mean the freedom of everyone to be enterprising?

Large corporations not only dominate our economy and our government, they also dominate the shaping of our children's minds. Never before in history have children grown up with their greatest influence coming from—not schools, churches or parents—but from institutions concerned primarily with selling them commodities.

As children pass through their formative years and go on to college they find that corporations also dominate our system of higher education. Look at photographs of the regents and trustees of all the colleges in the United States. The photos all look the same. Corporate and banking officials dominate the governing boards of our universities. This simple fact helps explain why there is a corporate-driven research agenda at most colleges, there are few connections between the college and the local community, and there are regular struggles over tuition increases that restrict access to higher education for working class youth.

Yet just as corporate domination of every sector of American society is being consolidated, broad sectors of the population are rising up to challenge that domination. The November 1999 protests in Seattle at the World Trade Organization meeting sent shock waves around the world and emboldened the anti-corporate movement to raise basic questions about how capital gets invested. The same grassroots movement that blocked the Multilateral Agreement on Investments (MAI), and stopped President Clinton from getting "fast-track" authority to negotiate trade deals, and mounted mass protests in Washington, D.C. at the April 2000 World Bank/IMF meetings, is now growing in both size and sophistication.

It is ironic but logical that residents of the richest country on earth, who have reaped the material rewards of U.S. institutions dominating the planet, are the very ones who are rejecting money values and shifting toward the life values that hold some potential for a transition to a sustainable and fair global economy.

WHAT DO AMERICANS THINK?

- 72 percent of Americans say corporations have too much power;[1]
- 74.1 percent of Americans say that we have a moral responsibility to be aware of inhumane conditions in factories that produce goods for U.S. markets;[2]
- 75.7 percent of Americans said they would pay $5 more for a $20 article of clothing to know that it was not produced under sweatshop conditions;[3]
- 52 percent of Americans said they agreed with the protesters in Seattle opposing the WTO in late 1999.[4]

1. "Too Much Corporate Power?" *Business Week*, September 11, 2000.
2. "Does the Public Care?" *Foreign Policy*, July/August 2001, p. 59.
3. *Ibid.*
4. "Business Week/Harris Poll: A Survey of Discontent," *Business Week*, December 27, 1999.

9

Spirituality vs. Mammon

The ideology of the free market—valuing commercialism above all else— goes against the great spiritual teachings of the world and is creating ethical bankruptcy.

The growing protests against the World Bank and the IMF are part of a larger paradigm shift taking place around the world. The shift away from money values toward life values is often strongest among well-educated people who are precisely the ones who have benefited most from the material abundance of capitalist industrialization. The dominant *quantitative* values—emphasizing material possessions—are increasingly challenged by a different set of *qualitative* values, emphasizing life-centered values such as human rights and protecting the environment. More and more people are seeing through the thin material values of the marketplace, realizing that the most important things in life cannot be purchased with money.

What do all the great spiritual leaders throughout history teach? Do they say amassing material wealth is the key to enlightenment? No, they teach precisely the opposite.

Confucius said: "The superior person knows what is right; the inferior person knows what will sell."

The Koran says: "As for those who hoard up gold and silver and do not spend the same in the service of Allah's cause, give them the tidings of painful sufferings."[1]

The Torah treats the human behavior known as covetousness—desiring the possessions of others—in totally negative terms. Yet today's promoters of the market ideology have enshrined covetousness as the core driving principle of human success.

The Bible says that "the love of money is the root of all evil."[2] It also says, "You cannot serve both God and mammon."[3]

Jesus preached strict nonviolence and even proposed loving one's enemies, yet he got violent one time, and what occupation did he choose to whip? It was bankers; the money-changers in the temple! So it is truthful to say that 99 percent of the protesters outside the World Bank headquarters are less violent than Jesus: we don't want to whip the bankers and throw their money on the ground, we want to change the rule-making and the structure of the global economy.

Social connectedness and responsibility—not individual material acquisition—have been key to all the great inspirational philosophies: the classical Chinese concept of *jen* (that which cannot stand the suffering of another); or the second commandment of Jesus which instructed us to "love thy neighbor as thy self."

In the contemporary world, Rev. Martin Luther King. Jr. described the key guiding principle of the civil rights movement this way: "Our political compass is love, and it always points toward solidarity."

The Cree Indians understood that there were more important things in life than money. They said:

> *Only when the last tree has died*
> *And the last river has been poisoned*

And the last fish has been caught
Will we realize that we cannot eat money.[4]

Yet look at what the dominant market ideology teaches: money is what matters, it is the way to measure success, and we should set policy according to the dictates of the market. An individual's success or a nation's development is measured *quantitatively* in terms of "how much stuff you have," rather than *qualitatively* in terms of your relations with other people and the natural world.

The authors of *Beyond the Limits* clarify the issue:

> People don't need enormous cars they need respect. They don't need closets full of clothes, they need to feel attractive and they need excitement and variety and beauty. People don't need electronic equipment: they need something worthwhile to do with their lives. People need identity, community, challenge, acknowledgement, love, and joy. To try to fill these needs with material things is to set up an unquenchable appetite for false solutions to real and never-satisfied problems. The resulting psychological emptiness is one of the major forces behind the desire for material growth.[5]

RICH MEDIA, POOR SPIRITS

The corporate-controlled media are a key mechanism debasing our values. We are deceived as to what the media really are. They are neither information media nor entertainment media. They are *commercial* media. They exist to make money. And they do that—*not* by selling tires and toothpaste to us "consumers"—they do it by selling *us* (access to our minds) to the corporate advertisers who pay the bills for all the major radio, TV, and print media. The corporate advertisers pay huge amounts for the privilege of penetrating our minds with a commodity consciousness that repeats the mantra: "buy more stuff."

We are not the consumers of the media, we are the product; it is the corporate advertisers who possess "consumer sovereignty." The consciousness of a self-governing citizen (the democratic ideal) is very different from the consciousness of a human commodity being marketed to corporate advertisers. The owners of the media do not want informed, thinking people; they want commodity junkies who will not rebel against their limited roles as workers/consumers.

Slavery is the buying and selling of whole human beings. The commercial media (using the public airwaves, *our* property!) buy and sell a part of a human being—attention, our consciousness. It is a far less brutal form of slavery than the historical version but it is still the selling of human beings.

Yet there is a positive side to the fact that the average person in the United States gets hit with an average of 3,000 commercial messages per day. This is proof that it is not normal or natural to orient our lives around buying commodities. If it *were* the natural, organic way for humans to behave, it wouldn't be necessary for the corporations to bombard us with so many commercial messages; they would occasionally say, "hey, remember to buy commodities" and we would all run off to the shopping mall. No, the natural focus for human beings is to orient our lives around love, caring, family, community, justice, and protecting the natural environment upon which all life depends. That is such a powerful drive that it takes constant commercial bombardment to cause us to forget it.

So do we subordinate life (people and nature) to the economy, or do we subordinate the economy to life? The correct choice for the sake of our children's children's children requires that we democratize the global economy. This gargantuan task has already begun in the form of thousands of grassroots organizations around the world who are redefining economics from the ground up.

NOTES

1. Surah 9: Verse 35.
2. Matthew, 6:24.
3. Timothy (I), 6:10.
4. David G. Mandelbaum, *The Plains Cree: An Ethnographic, Historical, and Comparative Study* (Regina: Canadian Plains Research Center, 1979).
5. Donella Meadows, Dennis Meadows, and Jorgen Randers, *Beyond the Limits* (Post Mills, VT: Chelsea Green, 1992).

People's Globalization to the Rescue

Élite globalization is being rejected by millions of people all over the world, and they are building a democratic alternative: bottom-up, people's globalization.

The democratic version of globalization could be called globalization-from-below or grassroots internationalism. This alternative vision for the planet is being constructed by diverse people and organizations who realize that our current definition of democracy is incomplete: when we allow huge corporations to buy control of the political process, and dominate global governing institutions, that is not real democracy.

Let's look at some of the dynamic social movements that make up the democratic version of globalization, keeping in mind that none of them, by themselves, are revolutionary. Only a mass movement that links many diverse interests can create revolution on a global scale.

The fair trade movement sells hundreds of millions of dollars worth of third world crafts and commodities (coffee, tea, chocolate, etc.) in first world markets with the goal—*not* of making first world entrepreneurs rich—but of providing a living wage and a more dignified existence to third world producers.

The fair trade labeling movement is making it easier for consumers to choose products produced with fair wages and dignity. When coffee consumers, for example, choose coffee with the TransFair USA, "fair trade certified" label on it, they can rest assured that the coffee growers were paid a living wage, received credit and technical assistance, were treated with respect, and grew their coffee in sustainable ways.[1]

Eco-labeling is also spreading because it allows consumers to channel dollars toward products produced in more environmentally sustainable ways.

We will some day have substantive labels on all products (similar to nutrition labeling on processed food) informing the consumer of the social and environmental impact of how each product was produced. The reason we don't have this already is not because of some technical difficulty; it is because the transnational corporations that dominate world markets do not want us to know the damage being done by their production processes.

Socially responsible investing has taken off like a rocket in the past two decades. Spurred by the anti-apartheid and environmental movements, socially responsible investing is gradually redefining the bottom-line away from just profit maximization toward including environmental sustainability and social accountability. Shareholder activism—voting stock in favor of corporate reform—is another area of socially responsible investing that challenges the corporate governance structure to expand corporate objectives beyond the financial bottom line to include social and environmental criteria.

Community currency organizations are defending local economies by creating local money that is accepted by small business but shunned by the large corporations. This helps slow the hemorrhaging of funds from the local economy due to the extractive nature of investment by transnational corporations.

The Tobin Tax—a proposal for a small tax on international currency transactions—is an idea which, if implemented, would extract wealth from the least productive sector of the global economy (currency speculation) and redirect the money toward the areas of greatest social and environmental need. It would also slow down the volatility of the currency exchange markets which tend to destabilize the economies of smaller nations.

Alternative communities/states such as Gaviotas, Colombia; Kerala, India; and Porto Alegre, Brazil are living proof that there are ways to solve problems in housing, transportation, literacy, and food availability by getting the decision-making process down closer to the people.

The growth of alternative models of ownership such as co-ops and Employee Stock Ownership Plans (ESOPs) reflect a desire by people of many cultures to democratize the ownership of capital and the control over work. Trade unions, religious groups, nonprofits, and community coalitions are experimenting with new forms of property ownership designed to protect the people's right to control their own communities. In the United States, for example, nonprofit organizations currently constitute some 6.5 percent of the U.S. economy, and cooperatives (47,000 nationwide) and worker-owned businesses (including 2,500 in which employees own the majority of stock shares) feature long-term ties to a community and are not likely to run away as so many corporations have done in recent years.

Thousands of micro-enterprise lending groups—based on the successful Grameen Bank in Bangladesh—have proliferated around the world in rich countries as well as poor countries. They are based on the understanding that capital is like horse manure: concentrated in one big pile it stinks, but spread out evenly it makes things grow. Part of the struggle to democratize the control of capital is to get capital into the hands of the people. While some leftists may denigrate this institutional model as nothing more than creating a larger sector of petit-bourgeois entrepreneurs, it is very powerful to see people enabled to work their way out of poverty through access to small amounts of credit.

There is a growing corporate accountability movement with many facets:

• The Mitsubishi boycott in which the Rainforest Action Network and other activist groups opposed to Mitsubishi's record of forest destruction forced Mitsubishi Electric and Mitsubishi Motor Sales to agree to changes in their environmental policies;

• An international boycott of ExxonMobil, attempting to force the company to change policies ranging from its polluting of the global climate to the way it treats gay and lesbian employees;

• Groups pressuring Nike to treat their Asian workers better; people criticizing Shell, Chevron, and other oil companies for their complicity with government repression in Nigeria;

• Civic groups attacking the tobacco companies for making billions of dollars selling a product that, when used as intended, kills the consumer;

• The Free Burma Coalition forcing transnational corporations to pull out of Burma because of the massive human rights abuses of Burma's military dictatorship;

• Anti-sweatshop groups forcing universities to sign on to the more radical of the two sweatshop monitoring associations, the Workers' Rights Consortium.

And the list could go on.

The corporate accountability movement is evolving to the systemic level: questioning the very nature of corporate empowerment. People are learning that corporations exist because we, the sovereign citizens, charter them through our state constitutions and give them a piece of our sovereignty. What can be given can be taken away, if enough citizens demand it.

There is an increasingly sophisticated international movement aimed at reforming or abolishing the World Bank, the International Monetary Fund, and the World Trade Organization, and replacing them with more democratic rule-making bodies for the global economy.

There is a diverse range of organizations working for a return-to-the-local in terms of citizen empowerment.[2] These efforts range across the political spectrum, yet they agree that as much decision-making as possible (political and economic) should take place at the local level, where people actually live. This is in sharp contrast to current trends in élite globalization.

The world's trade union movement is undergoing a double transformation. More and more unionists are realizing that organizing within a national context is no longer adequate for dealing with transnational corporations, and unions must increase their level of cross-border solidarity. Trade unions are also expanding their traditionally narrow shop-floor focus, and are replacing it with what might be called social unionism or community-based unionism, which seeks out alliances with churches, NGOs, and other organizations in civil society.[3]

The environmental movement is realizing that the commons—the air, water, and land that make up our common heritage—must be protected from being despoiled by narrow private interests. More and more environmentalists are moving beyond "end-of-pipeline" politics (standing outside the institutions of power trying to deflect the damaging effects of their policies) to focusing on changing the institutions and rules by which policy is made. More and more groups are bridging the traditional separation between environmental struggles and social justice struggles.

None of these movements are revolutionary by themselves because none are individually capable of replacing capitalism as a system. But each in its own way recognizes, at least inherently if not explicitly, that the system must move toward democratizing the way in which capital gets invested.

JUST A MARKET OR A JUST MARKET?

Around the world millions of people are realizing that the bulls-eye political issue is how capital gets invested. If you're talking about jobs, you've got to deal with how capital gets invested. If you're talking about environmental destruction, gender inequality, institutional racism, or immigration, you need to look at how capital gets invested.

Why do so many Mexican people risk their lives to come to the United States? Is it because of the bright lights of Los Angeles? No, these people are crossing that dangerous border because there are not enough well-paying jobs in Mexico. Why are there insufficient job opportunities in Mexico, a country rich in farmland, natural resources, capital, and creative people? Because the economy of Mexico has been run in the interests of local élites and their wealthy foreign allies in Washington and Wall Street. The structure of the economy was designed to *extract* wealth from the base and transfer it up and out.

So if we are going to get at the roots of these problems, we have to ask two questions about how capital gets invested.

(1) Who's sitting at the table? Is it a monocrop: all wealthy, corporate males, or is it biodiverse, representing all sectors of the bouquet that is humanity?

(2) What are the values governing how the capital gets invested? Is the central goal maximizing profits for large corporations? Or is the central goal meeting all human needs and saving the environment?

The World Bank and the IMF are fundamentally incapable of addressing these questions in a democratic manner. They have shown time and again that they cannot open themselves up to public participation and allow the poor majority to control how capital gets invested. They share so many interests with banks, corporations, and ruling élites, that no amount of tinkering with their rules and policies will convert them into democratic institutions.

These, and other global capitalist institutions such

as the World Trade Organization, need to be scrapped and replaced by a democratic process that includes representatives of the poor at all stages of planning and rule-making.

It is not the proper place of this author or any other privileged individual or group to tell less advantaged folks how to do "development." We can be advisors and provide technical assistance and help link grassroots groups across borders, but no one should be using large amounts of money to dictate to others how they structure their societies.

We should not expect that any one author can or should develop a blueprint for democratic institutions to replace the World Bank and the IMF. But in the concluding chapter of this book we suggest some basic principles and possible institutional directions for democratizing the distribution of capital on a global scale. Replacement institutions for the World Bank and the IMF will be developed through mass struggle on a global scale. Wealthy élites will implement limited reforms and try to maintain their grip on power while intensifying their propaganda to the effect that they really care about human rights and the environment. The movement for global justice will be challenged to respond in ways that push capital down toward the grassroots where it is most productive and most needed.

There *will* some day be a democratic global economy. The question is: will that take 15 years or 150 years? If it takes 150 years we are going to see a descent into barbarism that will make our current problems look like paradise in comparison.

NOTES

1. See the TransFair USA website at www.transfairusa.org.

2. Michael H. Shuman, *Going Local: Self-Reliant Communities in a Global Age* (New York: The Free Press, 1998).

3. See Kim Moody, *Workers in a Lean World: Unions in the International Economy* (London: Verso Books, 1997).

Building the Movement for a Democratic Global Economy

A basic human drive is to bond with other human beings. It is based on the visceral understanding that an individual cannot survive without other humans. The few cases of humans growing up outside of a social network are referred to as "feral children" (raised by wolves or other animals) and they are not really human: they can't talk or otherwise interact with humans. Also, look at the cases of children who were locked away for extended periods and deprived of human contact. These children are usually damaged permanently by this social deprivation.

The basic need for social solidarity finds expression in many forms: the euphoria of the sports arena, the camaraderie fostered by emotional religious services, the political ecstasy of mass movements that unite people around a cause (these can range from the mass movements in the United States for civil rights reform and an end to the war in Vietnam, to the recent mass mobilizations against corporate globalization). There is a transformative, euphoric feeling associated with being bonded to other people.

This basic need to experience solidarity—"complete unity, as of opinion, purpose, interest, feeling" (Webster's)—can either be manipulated by leaders seeking narrow goals, or it can be democratically debated and controlled by the people themselves to promote the broadest possible advance of human society.

Many political organizers have discovered that an intellectual analysis is not enough to mobilize large numbers of people for social change activism. It also requires emotional bonding. So the question for political activists is "Where's the passion?" As author and social critic Barbara Ehrenreich points out: "No matter how good the issues are or how appropriate the 'objective' conditions are ... you don't really get a movement that changes things in a big way unless it is fired by some of this passion."

REMOVING BARRIERS, BUILDING BRIDGES

In building social solidarity we need to identify barriers that keep us apart, and we need to devise bridges that can cross those barriers.

People are kept from feeling and acting in solidarity by real and imagined barriers. Most of us were raised in a society that taught us to (pre)judge each other as representatives of categories (male/female, rich/poor, white/color, gay/straight, etc.), rather than as unique individuals who may or may not comply with all the characteristics of the others who look or act like members of that category. Yet despite all the efforts of the fear-mongers, prejudice is increasingly discredited around the world: It is now seen as wrong, both politically and scientifically. Not withstanding the legislative and economic victories of the millionaire minority in recent years, prejudice can no longer be openly espoused without encountering derision and opposition.

That is why those promoting racism, sexism, and class, privilege must couch their arguments in pseudo-scientific rationales ascribing blame to the victims of oppression rather than to the social system that perpetrates the oppression. We have all heard these arguments: oppressed ethnic groups are lazy; the poor create poverty by having too many children; women's dependent social status is biologically determined; and the stupidity goes on and on.

We have heard these rationales so many times that we have become desensitized to their noxious effects. You can still hear well-meaning people justify top-down foreign aid with phrases such as, "if you give a man a fish you feed him for a day; if you teach him *how* to fish, you feed him for a lifetime." As if the problem were the ignorance of the poor! People who insist on blaming the victims while they hand out charity fish need to ask alternative questions such as: Who owns the lake? Who owns the bait, boats, and fishing gear? Who controls the global markets for fish?

This shift from questioning the integrity of the oppressed to questioning the structure and rules of power would help take us past charity consciousness to solidarity consciousness. Instead of asking the charity question, "How do we feed all the hungry people?" we should ask the solidarity question, "What changes do we need to make in the structures of economic and political power so that everyone can feed themselves?" The latter line of questioning leads to a far more dignified road to "development" than the traditional brand of altruism could ever produce.

It is instructive that the word *altruism* derives from

similar Latin roots as *alienation*—they both refer to a feeling of "other"ness; a separation of the speaker from the object of discussion. We should not see the oppressed as "other" because—given a different roll of the biological dice ("there but for fortune, go you and I")—we ourselves could be subject to the same injustice and misery as anyone else on the planet. As the playwright Julian Beck has said, "they" are you and I dressed differently.

GRASSROOTS INTERNATIONALISM: THE NEXT STAGE OF HUMAN SOLIDARITY

The great spiritual guides of many cultures have told us that we are supposed to love our neighbors as we love ourselves, we are to be our brothers' and sisters' "keepers" (as in protectors/comrades, not game wardens), and we should strive for unity among the human family (there is one race, the human race; or, as rock 'n roll legend Little Richard says, "All the races are God's bouquet.").

This is a beautiful ideology but the challenge confronting us is how to operationalize these sentiments in the day-to-day running of our institutions.

We can never achieve global social solidarity as long as those who make mass transit policy never ride the bus, those who make housing policy live in mansions, and those who make food policy are overweight from too much money and self-indulgence.

If we allow structures of unequal wealth and power to isolate and insulate the controllers of our institutions from feeling the impact of their policies, we will never fix what is wrong. The key question is *not* whether any particular leader is a moral person: if the structures of power and the rules of the game guarantee elitism and the separation of the rulers from the ruled (spread of gated communities?) no simple change in personnel at the top will change the outrageous injustice of an abundant world in which one child dies of hunger, on average, every few seconds.

Clearly, in order to change the massive disparities of wealth and power in the world we will need to mobilize magnitudes of people that have previously only been mobilized in times of war. How can we activate similar numbers to eliminate war and war-making machinery? How can we mobilize the massive numbers of people we will need to save the environment, to feed all the children, and to wipe out illiteracy?

The beginning of an answer is already visible on the horizon. People are increasingly identifying themselves as global citizens. They are breaking down barriers of race, nationality, gender, class and age to build unity with people who a generation ago would have been viewed as "other."

More and more people are realizing that we cannot afford the narrow-mindedness of nationalism. And it's not just geographical nationalism that is being superseded; people are also moving beyond gender "nationalism," race "nationalism," and religious "nationalism," They increasingly realize that identifying just with the group that looks, thinks, or acts like you will not cut it in a globalizing world. People are realizing that interest group politics—while necessary for establishing a group's own distinct self-definition—should only be a transitional stage to a "larger-tent" philosophy that is self-assured enough to link interest groups in ever-broader networks and coalitions. Just as individuals must subordinate their egos to group process in order for the group to succeed, organizations and interest groups must also subordinate their group egos to the needs of building the global mass movement.

BETTER THAN A BLUEPRINT

Many people have an understandable longing for a "plan" to run the world in a more just way. But we should focus our energies more on the process for producing a plan than on the plan itself.

Real global democracy will come—not in the form of some centralized supergovernment—but through a transnational federation of empowered local communities. These locally rooted, participatory institutions will constitute a global civil society in which technologies are mobilized—not to increase private profits—but to better empower the citizenry to communicate, debate, develop policies, and oversee the civil servants who implement the people's policy choices. If computer equipment and phone lines were made universally accessible, our brothers and sisters in the global south could engage us in regular dialogue about how we need to change the global economy. Questioning one's privilege requires opening oneself up to the otherness and anger of those without privilege. This planetary dialogue will prove to be the largest-scale social therapy ever attempted. Of course this sounds utopian. But utopian thinking, if linked to practical tactics, is a good thing, not a bad thing.

A prime operating principle for any global federation with popular legitimacy will be to push decision-making down as close to the local level as possible. Issues that are inherently global (e.g., climate change) will be decided by truly democratic global institutions that are accountable to the grassroots—in sharp contrast to the global institutions of today (World Bank, IMF, transnational corporations) whose policies run so counter to the popular interest that they must cloak their operations in secrecy.

While the exact shapes of future institutions are impossible for one person to predict, there are two areas in which we can guess with some certainty what the alternative global economic institutions will look like: principles and practices.

The principles of the new economic institutions will be based on rights established in the 1948 Universal Declaration of Human Rights. The right to eat, the right to a job, the right to adequate housing, the right to health care, are all guaranteed *on paper*, but few countries have fulfilled these rights *in practice* for all citizens. If the WTO can pass laws subordinating everything to commerce, then democratic global institutions can pass different laws that subordinate commerce to the goal of ensuring every human being's right to a dignified existence free of want. That is the challenge and the opportunity now facing the movement for global economic justice.

The practices of a people's global economy will seek nothing less than reversing the last 500 years of redistribution of wealth upward in the global class structure. This will be done with a range of programs designed to redirect the control of capital down to the grassroots, community level. Democratization of the economy requires more than consultation with the poor; it requires putting *control* over the capital investment process into the hands of the majority. As detailed in the previous chapter, there are already many institutions implementing policies that remove the market from its dominant role and replace it with democratic decision-making.

This future global democracy—now in its foundation-building stage—will eventually replace the current world order of profit and unaccountable power. The faster we can bring about the transition to a sustainable and democratically organized global economy the greater our chances of avoiding escalating social violence and the total collapse of biological systems upon which human society depends.

Although we need to treat our situation as an emergency, we also need long-term vision in constructing a new global economy based on life values instead of money values. I.F. Stone said that if you expect an answer to your question during your lifetime, you're not asking a big enough question. The masons who laid the first layer of the Great Wall of China knew that they would not see the final product of their work, but they still did very precise work. They understood that when you are laying the foundation of something large, you must do high-quality work because the future weight of the structure is going to rest on your efforts.

BUILDING THE MOVEMENT

At the most basic level, the problem confronting us

is that human consciousness is capable of creating "the other," whether this split is along lines of race, class, gender, political tactics (violence/nonviolence), or other divides. Categorizing people as the "other"—especially when it comes to ideological differences—allows you to avoid exposing your version of the truth to that person's version. This may be convenient but it is also cowardly. It ignores the simple fact that you usually learn more when testing your political theories against those who disagree with you than when you talk to people who share your perspective.

I am privileged to have respectful conversations with all sorts of people: mainstream people who trash "violent anarchists" without knowing any anarchists by name; anarchists who trash "liberal pacifists" without engaging them directly in dialogue. It strikes me that these people are doing essentially the same thing: they are labeling and then writing-off people they disagree with. But in building the movement, we are not trying to agree 100 percent with one another; we are simply trying to collaborate enough on practical and tactical levels so we can replace the existing institutions dominated by money values with new institutions dominated by life values.

So if we are going to build bridges among different sectors of the human bouquet, rather than building walls, then we need to find creative ways to reach out to sectors of the population that are not currently involved in the global justice movement.

We should strive to see the struggle—*not* as one opposed to particular individuals or groups of individuals—but as one opposed to systems/institutions/rules that create divisions within the life family (humans and other living things in harmony). So we need to change institutional structures that create unequal access to wealth and power, and a tendency to define the problem as some "other" that needs to be repressed.

One thing we can all do to build the global justice movement is to avoid self-marginalizing behavior: everything from sectarian ideology ("I'm more radical than you"), to bad breath or lack of social skills. How many times have you seen or heard of an organizer who had a good analysis of the evils of the system but hurt the movement because s/he didn't know how to treat people with respect during face-to-face interactions?

It is in our own self-interest to grow beyond our current individual perspectives. A good way to facilitate this is to be guided by the question: "What does the movement for global justice need from me right now?" If the answer is, build the *mass* movement, then we need to be constantly reaching out to new people, bringing them into a big-tent movement that will be called home by many different kinds of people.

We, the ever-expanding global justice movement, are building the foundation of a future global economy in which there will be not one starving child, and in which every child will have shoes and a school and medical care. We must believe that this is possible, and go out and change the world to make it a reality, and soon.

Are *you* ready?

Resources

There is a growing treasure trove of educational resources on the global economy and how we can change it. There are many good organizations and individuals working on these issues; we apologize to those of you we forgot to mention.

ORGANIZATIONS

• *World Bank Bond Boycott* An excellent campaign that links local action to global impact that helps trade unions, churches, colleges, local governments, and other institutions pass resolutions against buying World Bank bonds. Because the World Bank gets more than 80 percent of its funding from these bonds, the grassroots boycott of the bonds can exert real pressure on World Bank leaders. www.worldbankboycott.org (202) 299-0020

• *50 Years Is Enough Network*, (202) IMF-BANK (463-2265), www.50years.org

• *Alliance for Democracy*, (781) 894-1179, www.afd-online.org

• *Campaign for Labor Rights*, (202) 544-9355, www.summersault.com/~agj/clr/

• *Essential Information*, (202) 387-8030, www.essential.org

• Food First/Institute for Food and Development, (510) 654-4400, www.foodfirst.org

• *Focus on the Global South*, Bangkok, Thailand, 66-2-2187363, www.focusweb.org

• *Global Exchange*, (800) 497-1994, www.globalexchange.org

• *Independent Media Center Network*, (888) 686-9252, www.indymedia.org

• *Institute for Policy Studies*, (202) 234-9382, www.ips-D.C..org

• *International Forum on Globalization*, (415) 229-9350, www.ifg.org

• *Jobs with Justice*, (202) 434-1106, www.jwj.org

- *JustAct*, (415) 431-4204, www.justact.org
- *Public Citizen's Global Trade Watch/Citizens Trade Campaign* (202) 546-4996, www.tradewatch.org
- *Third World Network*, www.twnside.org.sg
- *Transnational Research and Action Center*, (415) 561-6568, www.corpwatch.org
- *Women's EDGE: Economic Development and Global Equality*, (202) 884-8396, www.womensedge.org
- *World Bank Bond Boycott Campaign*, (202) 299-0020, www.worldbankboycott.org

BOOKS

The Cancer Stage of Capitalism, John McMurtry (London: Pluto Press, 1999).

The Cult of Impotence: Selling the Myth of Powerlessness in the Global Economy, Linda McQuaig (New York: Viking, 1998).

The Future in the Balance, Walden Bello (Oakland, CA: Food First Books, 2001).

Good Taxes: The Case for Taxing Foreign Currency Exchange and Other Financial Transactions, Alex C. Michalos (Toronto: Dundurn Press, 1997).

Localization: A Global Manifesto, Colin Hines (London: Earthscan, 2000).

The No-Nonsense Guide to Globalization, Wayne Ellwood (London: Verso, 2001).

The No-Nonsense Guide to Fair Trade, David Ransom (London: Verso, 2001).

Taming Global Finance: New Thinking on Regulating Speculative Capital Marketes, Walden Bello, et al. eds., (New York: Zed Books, 2000).

PERIODICALS

Newsletter of the 50 Years Is Enough Network, (202) IMF-BANK, www.50years.org

KEVIN DANAHER

Multinational Monitor, (202) 234-5176, www.essential.org/monitor/

The Progressive Populist, (800) 732-4992, www.populist.com

Yes: A Journal of Positive Futures, (206) 842-0216, www.futurenet.org

RESOURCES FROM GLOBAL EXCHANGE

Democratizing the Global Economy: The Battle Against the World Bank and the International Monetary Fund, ed. by Kevin Danaher (Monroe, ME, Common Courage Press, 2001).

50 Years is Enough: The Case Against the World Bank and the International Monetary Fund, ed. by Kevin Danaher (Boston: South End Press, 1994).

Globalization in Our Own Front Yard. (24 pp.)

Whose Globalization?—These two half hour talks by Kevin Danaher will give you a clear contrast between the élite globalization promoted by the World Bank/IMF and the grassroots globalization of the global justice movement. (65 minutes)

Nine Arguments Against the World Bank and the IMF—This video by Kevin Danaher explains the arguments made in this book. (50 minutes)

Breaking the Bank—Produced in conjunction with the Independent Media Center. (72 minutes)

Global Exchange also offers dozens of informative audio tapes examining crucial international issues. Produced by David Barsamian's Alternative Radio, these programs feature Howard Zinn, Cornel West, Noam Chomsky, Ralph Nader, Lani Guinier, Angela Davis, Vandana Shiva, and GX's Kevin Danaher. They average 60 minutes in length.

For more information:

Global Exchange, 2017 Mission St., San Francisco, CA 94110, (800) 497-1994, www.globalexchange.org/store.

ABOUT THE AUTHORS

KEVIN DANAHER is a co-founder of Global Exchange, the San Francisco –based human rights organization. Danaher received his Ph.D. in sociology from the University of California at Santa Cruz, and has lectured at universities and to community organizations throughout the United States, from the World Affairs Council in Alaska to Dartmouth College in New Hampshire.

Dr. Danaher has appeared on television and radio shows around the country. He has published articles in the *Los Angeles Times*, the *San Francisco Chronicle*, the *International Herald Tribune*, *Harvard Educational Review*, the *Nation*, the *Progressive*, and many others.

Dr. Danaher has also written and edited many books dealing with U.S. foreign policy and the global economy. His most recent are *Democratizing the Global Economy: The Battle Against the World Bank and the IMF*; *Globalize This!: The Battle Against the World Trade Organization and Corporate Rule*; *Corporations Are Gonna Get Your Mama: Globalization and the Downsizing of the American Dream*; and *50 Years Is Enough: The Case Against the World Bank and the International Monetary Fund*.

ANURADHA MITTAL is the codirector of Food First/Institute for Food and Development Policy, a member-supported, nonprofit people's think tank and education-for-action center that is committed to establishing food as a fundamental human right. For more information see: www.foodfirst.org